# Why Foreign Aid?

RAND MCNALLY PUBLIC AFFAIRS SERIES

# Why Foreign

## Two Messages by President

BY

EDWARD C. BANFIELD

HOLLIS B. CHENERY

JOHN NUVEEN

HANS J. MORGENTHAU

MAX F. MILLIKAN

JOSEPH CROPSEY

# Aid?

## Kennedy and Essays

EDITED BY

ROBERT A. GOLDWIN

RAND McNALLY & COMPANY    ·    CHICAGO

RAND McNALLY PUBLIC AFFAIRS SERIES

*America Armed: Essays on United States Military Policy*
*A Nation of States: Essays on the American Federal System*
*Why Foreign Aid?*
*Political Parties, U.S.A.*
*100 Years of Emancipation*

# PREFACE

•

Although foreign aid has become a solidly established part of United States public policy during the course of the last two decades, in the last few years doubts as to its purposes and efficacy have not only persisted but have seemed to grow stronger and more widespread. Since no policy can be effective if it is unpopular, nor popular if its purposes are unclear, a new examination of the fundamental premises of foreign aid seems imperative, especially in its present and somewhat new form of assistance for the long-range development of underdeveloped countries.

There was little misunderstanding of the purpose of foreign aid when it was directed to the revival of the war-ravaged modern nations of Europe, but the question now is whether the same can be claimed for our programs of assistance to nations that have never had a modern economy. That is why the authors of the essays of this volume direct themselves primarily to consideration of one question: Why do we have a foreign aid program?

But this one question takes many forms. What are the purposes of foreign aid and can they be achieved? Should foreign aid programs be considered as primarily economic or political, short-run or long-term, for our sake or the sake of the recipient countries? (If it occurs to the reader that these need not be exclusive choices, and that the answer may be, "All of these," then the next question must be, are they truly compatible?) What are the standards of effort and success by which we can measure whether we are getting results commensurate with our expenditure? Is foreign aid justifiable on the ground of national interest; that is, is it but one more instrument of national policy? If so, can it be made to serve the national interest effectively? If not, is assistance to underdeveloped nations a moral duty that transcends the national limits of foreign policy as ordinarily understood?

Most of the authors of these essays argue that there is not at present an understanding of the basic task of economic assistance to underdeveloped nations clear enough and profound enough to serve as a reliable guide to policy. This volume is therefore offered in the hope that it will contribute to clarification of one of the most complex and troublesome issues of our time.

R. A. G.

April, 1963

# CONTENTS

●

The authors themselves are alone responsible for the opinions expressed and the policies recommended in their respective papers. The Public Affairs Conference Center is a nonpartisan, educational institution and as such takes no position on questions of public policy.

# THE EDITOR AND THE AUTHORS

●

ROBERT A. GOLDWIN

is Lecturer in Political Science and Director, Public Affairs Conference Center, University of Chicago. He is the editor of *Readings in World Politics*, 5th ed., 1959; *Readings in American Foreign Policy*, 4th ed., 1959; and *Readings in Russian Foreign Policy*, 3rd ed., 1959.

EDWARD C. BANFIELD

is Professor of Government, Harvard University, and a staff member of the Joint Center for Urban Studies of the Massachusetts Institute of Technology and Harvard University. His fields of study include urban politics and city planning. He is the author of *Government Project*, 1951; *Politics, Planning and the Public Interest*, 1955 (with Martin Meyerson); *Government and Housing in Metropolitan Areas*, 1958 (with Morton Grodzins); *The Moral Basis of a Backward Society*, 1958; and *Political Influence*, 1960.

HOLLIS B. CHENERY

is Assistant Administrator for Program, Agency for International Development (AID), Department of State. Formerly Professor of Economics at Stanford University, he has served with the Economic Cooperation Administration (ECA) and as Chief of the Program Division of the Mutual Security Administration. He is the co-author of *Arabian Oil*, 1949, and *Interindustry Economics*, 1959.

# The Editor and the Authors

JOHN NUVEEN

a Director of John Nuveen & Company, investment bankers, was the former Chief of the ECA Missions to Greece and Belgium. He is a Director of the American Friends of the Middle East and a Trustee of the University of Chicago.

HANS J. MORGENTHAU

is Professor of Political Science and Director of the Center for the Study of American Foreign and Military Policy, University of Chicago. His books include *Scientific Man* vs. *Power Politics*, 1946; *Politics Among Nations*, 1948 (3rd ed., 1960); *In Defense of the National Interest*, 1951; *Dilemmas of Politics*, 1958; *The Purpose of American Politics*, 1960; and *Politics in the Twentieth Century* (3 vols.), 1962.

MAX F. MILLIKAN

is Professor of Economics and Director of the Center of International Studies, Massachusetts Institute of Technology. He headed the Kennedy task force that recommended establishment of the Peace Corps and also was a consultant on foreign aid programs during the Eisenhower and Truman administrations. His books include *A Proposal—Key to a More Effective Foreign Policy*, 1957 (with W. W. Rostow), and *The Emerging Nations—Their Growth and United States Policy*, 1961 (editor and co-author with D. L. M. Blackmer).

JOSEPH CROPSEY

is Assistant Professor of Political Science, University of Chicago. His fields of specialization are economics and political philosophy. He is the author of *Polity and Economy*, 1957, and co-editor (with Leo Strauss) and joint author of *History of Political Philosophy*, 1963.

# President John F. Kennedy

●

# FOREIGN AID, 1961*

*To the Congress of the United States:*

This Nation must begin any discussion of "foreign aid" in 1961 with the recognition of three facts:

1. Existing foreign aid programs and concepts are largely unsatisfactory and unsuited for our needs and for the needs of the underdeveloped world as it enters the sixties.

2. The economic collapse of those free but less-developed nations which now stand poised between sustained growth and economic chaos would be disastrous to our national security, harmful to our comparative prosperity, and offensive to our conscience.

3. There exists, in the 1960's, a historic opportunity for a major economic assistance effort by the free industrialized nations to move more than half the people of the less-developed nations into self-sustained economic growth, while the rest move substantially closer to the day when they, too, will no longer have to depend on outside assistance.

## I

Foreign aid—America's unprecedented response to world challenges—has not been the work of one party or one administration. It has moved forward under the leadership of two great Presidents —Harry Truman and Dwight Eisenhower—and drawn its support from forward-looking members of both political parties in the Congress and throughout the Nation.

* Selections from the Message of the President to the Congress, on the subject of foreign aid, transmitted on March 22, 1961. Reprinted from *The Department of State Bulletin*, April 10, 1961.

## President John F. Kennedy

Our first major foreign aid effort was an emergency program of relief—of food and clothing and shelter—to areas devastated by World War II. Next we embarked on the Marshall plan—a towering and successful program to rebuild the economies of Western Europe and prevent a Communist takeover. This was followed by point 4—an effort to make scientific and technological advances available to the people of developing nations. And recently the concept of development assistance, coupled with the OECD (Organization for Economic Cooperation and Development), has opened the door to a united free world effort to assist the economic and social development of the less-developed areas of the world.

To achieve this new goal we will need to renew the spirit of common effort which lay behind our past efforts—we must also revise our foreign aid organization, and our basic concepts of operation to meet the new problems which now confront us. For no objective supporter of foreign aid can be satisfied with the existing program—actually a multiplicity of programs. Bureaucratically fragmented, awkward and slow, its administration is diffused over a haphazard and irrational structure covering at least four departments and several other agencies. The program is based on a series of legislative measures and administrative procedures conceived at different times and for different purposes, many of them now obsolete, inconsistent, and unduly rigid and thus unsuited for our present needs and purposes. Its weaknesses have begun to undermine confidence in our effort both here and abroad. The program requires a highly professional skilled service, attracting substantial numbers of high-caliber men and women capable of sensitive dealing with other governments, and with a deep understanding of the process of economic development. However, uncertainty and declining public prestige have all contributed to a fall in the morale and efficiency of those employees in the field who are repeatedly frustrated by the delays and confusions caused by overlapping agency jurisdictions and unclear objectives. Only the persistent efforts of those dedicated and hard-working public servants, who have kept the program going, managed to bring some success to our efforts overseas.

In addition, uneven and undependable short-term financing has weakened the incentive for the long-term planning and self-help by the recipient nations which are essential to serious economic development. The lack of stability and continuity in the program—the necessity to accommodate all planning to a yearly deadline—when combined with a confusing multiplicity of American aid agencies within a single nation abroad—have reduced the effectiveness of our own assistance and made more difficult the task of setting realistic targets and sound standards. Piecemeal projects, hastily designed to match the rhythm of the fiscal year are no substitute for orderly long-term planning. The ability to make long-range commitments has enabled the Soviet Union to use its aid program to make developing nations economically dependent on Russian support—thus advancing the aims of world communism.

Although our aid programs have helped to avoid economic chaos and collapse, and assisted many nations to maintain their independence and freedom—nevertheless, it is a fact that many of the nations we are helping are not much nearer sustained economic growth than they were when our aid operation began. Money spent to meet crisis situations or short-term political objectives while helping to maintain national integrity and independence has rarely moved the recipient nation toward greater economic stability.

## II

In the face of these weaknesses and inadequacies—and with the beginning of a new decade of new problems—it is proper that we draw back and ask with candor a fundamental question: Is a foreign aid program really necessary? Why should we not lay down this burden which our Nation has now carried for some 15 years?

The answer is that there is no escaping our obligations: our moral obligations as a wise leader and good neighbor in the interdependent community of free nations—our economic obligations as the wealthiest people in a world of largely poor people, as a nation no longer dependent upon the loans from abroad that once helped us develop our own economy—and our political obligations as the single largest counter to the adversaries of freedom. To fail to meet those obligations now would be disastrous; and, in the long run, more expensive. For widespread poverty and chaos lead to a collapse of existing political and social structures which would

3

inevitably invite the advance of totalitarianism into every weak and unstable area. Thus our own security would be endangered and our prosperity imperiled. A program of assistance to the underdeveloped nations must continue because the Nation's interest and the cause of political freedom require it.

We live at a very special moment in history. The whole southern half of the world—Latin America, Africa, the Middle East, and Asia—are caught up in the adventures of asserting their independence and modernizing their old ways of life. These new nations need aid in loans and technical assistance just as we in the northern half of the world drew successively on one another's capital and know-how as we moved into industrialization and regular growth.

But in our time these new nations need help for a special reason. Without exception they are under Communist pressure. In many cases, that pressure is direct and military. In others, it takes the form of intense subversive activity designed to break down and supersede the new—and often frail—modern institutions they have thus far built.

But the fundamental task of our foreign aid program in the 1960's is not negatively to fight communism: Its fundamental task is to help make a historical demonstration that in the twentieth century, as in the nineteenth—in the southern half of the globe as in the north—economic growth and political democracy can develop hand in hand.

In short we have not only obligations to fulfill, we have great opportunities to realize. We are, I am convinced, on the threshold of a truly united and major effort by the free industrialized nations to assist the less-developed nations on a long-term basis. Many of these less-developed nations are on the threshold of achieving sufficient economic, social, and political strength and self-sustained growth to stand permanently on their own feet. The 1960's can be—and must be—the crucial "decade of development"—the period when many less-developed nations make the transition into self-sustained growth—the period in which an enlarged community of free, stable, and self-reliant nations can reduce world tensions and insecurity. This goal is in our grasp if, and only if, the other industrialized nations now join us in developing with the recipients a set of commonly agreed criteria, a set of long-range

4

goals, and a common undertaking to meet those goals, in which each nation's contribution is related to the contributions of others and to the precise needs of each less-developed nation. Our job, in its largest sense, is to create a new partnership between the northern and southern halves of the world, to which all free nations can contribute, in which each free nation must assume a responsibility proportional to its means.

We must unite the free industrialized nations in a common effort to help those nations within reach of stable growth get under-way. And the foundation for this unity has already been laid by the creation of the OECD under the leadership of President Eisenhower. Such a unified effort will help launch the economies of the newly developing countries "into orbit"—bringing them to a stage of self-sustained growth where extraordinary outside assistance is not required. If this can be done—and I have every reason to hope it can be done—then this decade will be a significant one indeed in the history of freemen.

But our success in achieving these goals, in creating an environment in which the energies of struggling peoples can be devoted to constructive purposes in the world community—and our success in enlisting a greater common effort toward this end on the part of other industrialized nations—depends to a large extent upon the scope and continuity of our own efforts. If we encourage recipient countries to dramatize a series of short-term crises as a basis for our aid—instead of depending on a plan for long-term goals—then we will dissipate our funds, our good will, and our leadership. Nor will we be any nearer to either our security goals or to the end of the foreign aid burden.

In short, this Congress at this session must make possible a dramatic turning point in the troubled history of foreign aid to the underdeveloped world. We must say to the less-developed nations, if they are willing to undertake necessary internal reform and self-help—and to the other industrialized nations, if they are willing to undertake a much greater effort on a much broader scale—that we then intend during this coming decade of development to achieve a decisive turnaround in the fate of the less-developed world, looking toward the ultimate day when all nations can be self-reliant and when foreign aid will no longer be needed.

However, this will not be an easy task. The magnitude of the problems is staggering. In Latin America, for example, population growth is already threatening to outpace economic growth —and in some parts of the continent living standards are actually declining. In 1945 the population of our 20 sister American Republics was 145 million. It is now greater than that of the United States, and by the year 2000, less than 40 years away, Latin American population will be 592 million, compared with 312 million for the United States. Latin America will have to double its real income in the next 30 years simply to maintain already low standards of living. And the problems are no less serious or demanding in the other developing areas of the world. Thus to bring real economic progress to Latin America and to the rest of the less-developed world will require a sustained and united effort on the part of the Latin American Republics, the United States, and our free world allies.

This will require leadership, by this country in this year. And it will require a fresh approach—a more logical, efficient, and successful long-term plan—for American foreign aid. I strongly recommend to the Congress the enactment of such a plan, as contained in a measure to be sent shortly to the Congress and described below.

### III

If our foreign aid funds are to be prudently and effectively used, we need a whole new set of basic concepts and principles:

1. Unified administration and operation. . . .
2. Country plans—a carefully thought-through program tailored to meet the needs and the resource potential of each individual country. . . .
3. Long-term planning and financing. . . .
4. Special emphasis on development loans repayable in dollars. . . .
5. Special attention to those nations most willing and able to mobilize their own resources, make necessary social and economic reforms, engage in long-range planning, and make the other efforts necessary if these are to reach the stage of self-sustaining growth. . . .

## IV

I propose that our separate and often confusing aid programs be integrated into a single administration. . . .

## V

But new organization is not enough. We need a new working concept.

At the center of the new effort must be national development programs. It is essential that the developing nations set for themselves sensible targets; that these targets be based on balanced programs for their own economic, educational, and social growth—programs which use their own resources to the maximum. If planning assistance is required, our own aid organization will be prepared to respond to requests for such assistance, along with the International Bank for Reconstruction and Development and other international and private institutions. Thus, the first requirement is that each recipient government seriously undertake to the best of its ability on its own those efforts of resource mobilization, self-help, and internal reform—including land reform, tax reform, and improved education and social justice—which its own development requires and which would increase its capacity to absorb external capital productively.

These national development programs—and the kind of assistance the free world provides—must be tailored to the recipients' current stage of development and their foreseeable potential. A large infusion of development capital cannot now be absorbed by many nations newly emerging from a wholly underdeveloped condition. Their primary need at first will be the development of human resources, education, technical assistance, and the groundwork of basic facilities and institutions necessary for further growth. Other countries may possess the necessary human and material resources to move toward status as developing nations, but they need transitional assistance from the outside to enable them to mobilize those resources and move into the more advanced stage of development where loans can put them on their feet. Still others already have the capacity to absorb and effectively utilize substantial investment capital.

Finally, it will be necessary, for the time being, to provide grant assistance to those nations that are hard pressed by external or internal pressure so that they can meet those pressures and maintain their independence. In such cases it will be our objective to help them, as soon as circumstances permit, make the transition from instability and stagnation to growth; shifting our assistance as rapidly as possible from a grant to a development loan basis. For our new program should not be based merely on reaction to Communist threats or short-term crises. We have a positive interest in helping less-developed nations provide decent living standards for their people and achieve sufficient strength, self-respect, and independence to become self-reliant members of the community of nations. And thus our aid should be conditioned on the recipients' ability and willingness to take the steps necessary to reach that goal. . . .

## VI

A program based on long-range plans instead of short-run crises cannot be financed on a short-term basis. Long-term authorization, planning, and financing are the key to the continuity and efficiency of the entire program. If we are unwilling to make such a long-term commitment, we cannot expect any increased response from other potential donors or any realistic planning from the recipient nations.

I recommend, therefore, an authorization for the new aid agency of not less than 5 years, with borrowing authority also for 5 years to commit and make dollar repayable loans within the limits spelled out below. No other step would be such a clear signal of our intentions to all the world. No other step would do more to eliminate the restrictions and confusions which have rendered the current foreign aid program so often ineffective. No other step would do more to help obtain the service of top-flight personnel. And in no other way can we encourage the less-developed nations to make a sustained national effort over a long-term period.

For, if we are to have a program designed to brighten the future, that program must have a future. Experience has shown that long-range needs cannot be met evenly and economically by a series of 1-year programs. Close consultation and cooperation with the Congress and its committees will still be essential, including an annual review of the program. And we will still need annual appropriations of those amounts needed to meet requirements for which dollar repayable loans would be unsuitable. These appropriations should be available until spent in order to avoid any wasteful rush to obligate funds at the end of a fiscal year.

The new continuity and flexibility this kind of long-term authority will bring cannot help but result in more productive criteria, a greater effort on the part of the developing nations, greater contributions from our more prosperous allies, more solid results, and real long-run economy to the taxpayers. The new emphasis on long-term plans and realistic targets will give both the Congress and the Executive a better basis for evaluating the validity of our expenditures and progress.

\* \* \*

## IX

. . . Assistance to our fellow nations is a responsibility which has been willingly assumed and fashioned by two great Presidents in the past, one from each party—and it has been supported by the leaders of both parties in both Houses who recognized the importance of our obligations.

I believe the program which I have outlined is both a reasonable and sensible method of meeting those obligations as economically and effectively as possible. I strongly urge its enactment by the Congress, in full awareness of the many eyes upon us—the eyes of other industrialized nations, awaiting our leadership for a stronger united effort—the eyes of our adversaries, awaiting the weakening of our resolve in this new area of international struggle—the eyes of the poorer peoples of the world, looking for hope and help, and needing an incentive to set realistic long-range goals—and, finally, the eyes of the American people, who are fully aware of their obligations to the sick, the poor, and the hungry, wherever they may live. Thus, without regard to party lines, we shall take this step not as Republicans or as Democrats but as leaders of the free world. It will both befit and benefit us to take this step boldly. For we are launching a decade of development on which will depend, substantially, the kind of world in which we and our children shall live.

## Edward C. Banfield

●

# AMERICAN FOREIGN AID DOCTRINES

This essay[1] examines critically the premises of American foreign aid doctrines. By foreign aid (or simply "aid") is meant technical assistance and loans and grants to underdeveloped countries for nonmilitary purposes. Aid programs may, of course, bear little resemblance to the doctrines by which they are justified; but it is *doctrines*, not *programs*, that are under discussion here.

The essay is in three parts. The first discusses the doctrines which place the ultimate justification of aid in its contribution to national defense. The second discusses those which place it on other grounds (altruism, the moral law, and improvement of American life). The last part appraises the general character of the discussion about aid and endeavors to show that the nature of American democracy makes a rational approach to the subject impossible.

### I. Aid Justified by National Security

Those who find the ultimate justification for aid in its contribution to national security rely upon one or another of two incompatible doctrines. One doctrine asserts that the security purpose can be served by using aid to transform the fundamental character of the culture and institutions of the recipient country. The other takes the fundamental character of the recipient society as given and without seeking to change the culture or institutions of the country endeavors to achieve the purpose by influencing either its government or its public opinion. In this part of the essay, these

[1] Adapted from my article in *Public Policy*, C. J. Friedrich and Seymour Harris, eds., Harvard University Press, 1961. A revised and elaborated version has been published as a pamphlet by the American Enterprise Institute, Washington, D.C., 1963.

two doctrines will be discussed in turn and then the logical alternative to both (that is, no aid at all) will be considered.

## THE DOCTRINE OF INDIRECT INFLUENCE

One widely held view, which I will call the doctrine of indirect influence, asserts that aid can bring about in the outlook and institutions of the underdeveloped countries changes which will encourage the spread of freedom and democracy, thereby promoting peace and ultimately serving the vital security interest of the United States. Max F. Millikan and W. W. Rostow, who advance this argument in their influential book, *A Proposal*,[2] say that it is a serious misconception to believe that the mere creation of wealth will satisfy people's expectations; "some" increase of wealth is essential, they say, but the real importance of aid is that it will set off social, political, and psychological changes that will energize the society, point it in the direction of democracy, and incline it toward peace.

To estimate the likelihood of achieving the end ultimately sought (the greater security of the United States) in the manner prescribed by this doctrine, one must make judgments of four separate probabilities: (1) that aid will raise incomes by at least the minimum that is necessary for the other, energizing changes to occur; (2) that these changes (social, political, and psychological) will lead to freedom and democracy; (3) that freedom and democracy will lead to peace; and (4) that peace will serve the vital defense interests or the security interests of the United States. Let us consider these assumptions one by one.

1. The increase in wealth that is necessary must occur not simply in aggregate national incomes but in the actual incomes of ordinary men. Three factors are therefore involved: the productivity of the economy, the size of the population, and the evenness with which income is distributed. In most parts of the underdeveloped world all three of these factors will have to change.

Aggregate income has been increasing in most underdeveloped countries, but the gains have been offset, or nearly so, by increases

[2] New York: Harper and Brothers, 1957.

of population. Although their aggregate incomes are rising, the underdeveloped countries have not increased their per capita food supplies very significantly. P. N. Rosenstein-Rodan has estimated that if the underdeveloped countries get all the aid they can absorb, if they use it reasonably well, and if their populations increase by one-fourth, their gross national product may rise from an average of $140 per capita in 1961 to $192 in 1976.[3] Whether, even assuming no further rise in the "aspiration level" of the underdeveloped countries, this would be enough to change their outlook and institutions profoundly may well be doubted.

If one believes that modernization of the economies of the underdeveloped areas (not merely "some" improvement in their levels of living) will be required to produce the social and psychological effects that are sought, the case is even more discouraging. Some societies may never enter fully into modern ways. The American Indian, for example, has had extensive aid for decades, but he is still in most cases very far from belonging to the modern world.[4]

It is at least plausible to suppose that certain cultural prerequisites must be met in order for self-sustaining economic development to occur. One such prerequisite is probably the presence in the society of at least a few people who have the talents and incentives to organize, innovate, and take risks. Other prerequisites (which, incidentally, probably must be met in order for such a class to arise or to function effectively) are: widespread desire for material improvement, widespread belief that economic activity is worthy of respect, willingness to cooperate to some extent for the common welfare, and ability to maintain a certain degree of political stability. All of these prerequisites are critically lacking in the underdeveloped countries.

Where cultural conditions do not allow of it, economic development will not take place, no matter how much aid is given. On the other hand, where cultural conditions are right for it, development will occur rapidly in the absence of any aid. Japan and

---

[3] See Max F. Millikan and Donald L. M. Blackmer, eds., *The Emerging Nations* (Boston: Little, Brown, 1961), p. 154.

[4] See Frank A. Tinker, "The Navaho Experience," *Challenge*, December 1960, pp. 26–30.

Russia both developed rapidly without aid. No country is too poor to accumulate capital if its people are disposed to save and to invest, and the technical knowledge of the Western world is easily available to the underdeveloped countries—indeed, could not be withheld from them—if they are willing to avail themselves of it. Where populations have a "will" not to propagate excessively, the population problem will solve itself; where they do not have such a will, nothing much can be done about the population problem. The existence of a cheap and effective oral contraceptive does not put it within the power of a government—certainly not of our government—to reduce births among people who do not want to reduce them.

Aid doctrine tends greatly to overvalue the importance of both technical assistance and foreign capital in the development process. Only in the most backward countries can either make a crucial difference, and it is in these countries, of course, that the prospects of bringing about development are poorest. In countries like Mexico, where the likelihood of ultimate success is good, outside aid is not necessary in order for development to occur at what the leaders of the countries consider to be a satisfactory rate. Mexico, for example, has not accepted any aid. It is true that there is an important middle group of countries—India is a conspicuous example—which can absorb large amounts of aid and which also show fair promise of eventual development.[5] Nevertheless, there is in general an element of perversity in the situation: the more aid can be absorbed, the poorer the prospects for its eventual success.

There is also some possibility, as Milton Friedman has emphasized,[6] that aid may be so misapplied as to stifle initiative and

[5] Max Millikan's comment on this statement (p. 93 of this volume) exhibits more optimism than the case seems to warrant. That India *can* absorb large amounts of aid does not imply that the aid we have given, or might give, would actually contribute to her economic development. In fact, as I remark in the text below, India has used the opportunity afforded by our aid to increase her arms expenditures by at least an equivalent amount. Most of this arms expenditure contributes little or nothing to her economic development. If, as seems to be the case, our aid has simply enabled India to buy arms abroad, it has been (at least from the standpoint of our stated purposes in giving it to her) completely wasted.

[6] "Foreign Economic Aid: Means and Objectives," *The Yale Review*, Summer 1958.

entrepreneurship, thereby reducing the rate of growth to less than it would be if there were no aid at all.

Even if it does begin, economic development may not last very long or get very far. Continued growth, David McCord Wright has pointed out,[7] involves discovery and use of new ideas. The developing society must produce a social outlook, institutions, and economic organization which, generation after generation, will bring to the fore men who will produce new ideas. That such men come to the fore in one generation, Wright observes, is no guarantee that they will in the next. The long-run economic prospect, therefore, is very uncertain in any society, including of course a highly developed one like our own.

2. Even if economic growth does occur it will not necessarily lead to the spread of freedom and democracy. If what is meant by these is "respect for the individual" and its expression in some form of "government by discussion," there is no basis for optimism. Respect for the individual is unique to the Judaeo-Christian tradition, and in the underdeveloped parts of the world, where the worthlessness of the individual human life is an obvious fact of everyday experience, the concept of the dignity of man is not likely to be generally intelligible for generations to come.

If by "democracy" is meant something much less—that institutions are representative in the sense that they take some account of the wants and interests of the major elements of the population —then the outlook is better. But democracy, even in this very attenuated sense, will probably be of slow growth. Political institutions cannot be copied in the way technical practices can. It took the West several hundred years to arrive at its imperfect democracy; the underdeveloped areas may perhaps learn something from this experience, but, even so, they are not likely to do in decades what took us centuries.

The outlook for democracy is best in the cultures which share our fundamental moral premises. But even in Latin America, which has participated in Western civilization for 400 years, its prospects, short run or long run, are not encouraging.

[7] "Stages of Growth *vs.* The Growth of Freedom," *Fortune*, December 1959.

There is, indeed, much reason to expect that economic development, to the extent that it occurs, will prove incompatible with freedom and democracy. The spread of literacy, an indispensable accompaniment of economic growth, hastens the decay of tradition and other forms of authority. As Millikan and Rostow observe,

> The education which accompanies economic change contributes to unrest. People who can't read can't be subverted by literature. Once they can read, the process of widening knowledge and changing ideas of what the world is like and what is possible in it proceeds with great rapidity.[8]

In India, Asia, Africa, and Latin America, according to Bert F. Hoselitz and Myron Weiner, the relatively developed regions have shown themselves most prone to violence.[9]

The realistic question is not whether democracy can be brought into being in the foreseeable future in the underdeveloped countries —the answer almost everywhere is clearly, "No"—but whether there can be brought into being political systems that are capable of modernizing the countries at all. "No new state," Edward A. Shils has written, "can modernize itself and remain or become liberal and democratic without an elite of force of character, intelligence, and high moral qualities." Very few of the underdeveloped countries, he adds, have such elites; those that do have them may under favorable circumstances enjoy democracy that is to some extent tutelary, and in time, if the elite has a very powerful will to be democratic, the enormous gap between it and the masses of the population may be overcome. The less democratic and much more probable alternatives will not, he thinks, provide stable government at all:

> The alternatives are disorderly oligarchies, each promising and aspiring to maintain order and to modernize, but doing so only by sweeping the disorder temporarily into a box from which it recurrently springs out into full strength. The totalitarian oligarchy by the ruthlessness of its elite and by the vigor of its party machine as well as by the organiza-

---

[8] *A Proposal*, p. 22.
[9] "Economic Development and Political Stability," *Dissent*, Spring 1961.

tional and material aid which it would get from the Soviet Union, would appear to have the best chance to maintain itself, once it gets into power. But it too would have to compromise markedly with the human materials which traditional society gives it. It could build monuments and suppress open dissatisfaction but it could not realize its ideal.[10]

Some of the measures which may be necessary (or, more likely, which may be *thought* necessary) to induce rapid economic development are likely to discourage the growth of democracy. If a government thinks that the amount of voluntary saving is not enough to produce the rate of development that is sought, it is likely to use fraud or force to increase the amount of savings. Ruthless dictatorship will be defended as the only way, or the fastest and hence, in the long run, the least painful way to bring about self-sustained economic growth and modernization.

Other tendencies toward totalitarianism will be encouraged by the new technology of communications. For the first time in history it is now possible to rule a vast area by propaganda. People too poor to be ruled by force (force requires a police organization, something expensive to maintain) may now be ruled by radio and television, provided, of course, that those in control are skilled in playing upon the emotions of the masses. Whether "constructive" appeals (for example, for national crusades against poverty, disease, and ignorance) will prove as useful as campaigns of hate directed against the white, the capitalist, the foreigner, and the American, may well be doubted. As compared to the Communists, the West is at a great and probably hopeless disadvantage in the propaganda war. The Marxist ideology, as Adam B. Ulam has written,[11] is a *natural* one for backward societies because it provides what is, from the standpoint of people undergoing transition from pre-industrial to industrial society, an intelligible account of their experience. Democracy and freedom are too foreign to the experience of backward peoples to make sense to them.

[10] "Political Developments in the New States," *Comparative Studies in Society and History*, Vol. II (1960), pp. 407 and 410.
[11] *The Unfinished Revolution* (New York: Random House, 1960), Ch. VII.

In some of the underdeveloped countries the religion of nationalism is a dominant force. The leaders of these countries, and perhaps the people as well, are moved less by a desire for better living standards than by an urge to create a mystic bond, to assert the glory of the nation, and to demonstrate the superiority of the chosen people to all others. Where there is fervent nationalism, hate for the white man, the Westerner, indeed for all foreigners, is indispensable to the making of the new nation. Our enmity may (as Castro seems to think) be more valuable than our friendship in unleashing the energies by which a regime can maintain itself in power and, perhaps, make a nation.

3. Even if aid leads to economic development and even if economic development leads to freedom and democracy, peace may not be promoted. Disparities in the wealth of nations do not cause wars: poor, pre-industrial nations do not attack rich, industrial ones. Nor does a high level of economic and political development give any assurance at all that a nation will not be aggressive if it can be so with impunity. Millikan and Rostow have no basis for believing either that democratic societies "can be relied upon not to generate conflict because their own national interests parallel ours and because they are politically healthy and mature," or that as nations "gain confidence" they become easier to deal with.[12] The Soviet Union is a confident nation, and all the more dangerous for that. What counts is not the "maturity" or "confidence" of nations but their relative power and the purposes for which they would use that power.

There is even reason to think that our aid may already have been a cause of one war and that it may be leading to others. It is arguable that Israel could not have attacked Egypt if we had not given her aid. Similarly, the arms race between India and Pakistan seems to have been touched off by our aid to India; in any case, it is being financed on both sides by us. (We give nonmilitary aid to India, but this frees Indian funds for the purchase of arms. For several years India's military spending has offset, or somewhat more than offset, the amount of our aid.)

[12] *A Proposal*, pp. 4 and 32.

4. Even if the ultimate effect of aid were to make the countries in question entirely peaceful, our security might not be enhanced thereby and it might even be jeopardized. It would not be enhanced if the threat of nuclear retaliation is enough to protect us: war-like nations are no more dangerous than peaceable ones when the price of aggression is obliteration. Our security would actually be reduced by the peaceableness of these countries if the alternative (an unlikely one, to be sure) were that they would risk war in support of us. "Aggressive" countries in other words, might in some circumstances be preferable to peaceable ones from the standpoint of American security interests, provided, of course, that they were aggressive *on our side*.

The confidence one has in the doctrine of indirect influence will depend, then, upon the assessments one makes of each of these probabilities. If (to assign numbers for illustrative purposes only) there is one chance in ten that aid will produce economic growth, one chance in ten that economic growth will produce freedom and democracy, one chance in ten that democracy will produce peace, and one chance in ten that peace will add to our security, then the chance that aid will serve our national interest (in the manner prescribed) is one in ten thousand.

Whatever outcome one comes to, it is necessary to consider the element of time. It is wildly optimistic to think that the results intended can be secured in less than a generation or two. What, then, is the value of these results on the most optimistic estimate of them for dealing with the crisis of today and tomorrow? Even if it were absolutely certain that aid would produce all the results sought, it would be wise not to extend it if the results could not accrue in time to help us in the present crisis and if the giving of aid in the manner prescribed by the doctrine of indirect influence would prevent us from taking measures that might be effective in the short run.

### THE DOCTRINE OF DIRECT INFLUENCE

The doctrine of direct influence, that is, that aid should make its effect directly by influencing governments or public opinions and not indirectly by transforming cultures and institutions, takes several distinct forms:

## American Foreign Aid Doctrines

*1. Quid Pro Quo.* The aid is part of a bargain between two governments in which there are clearly specified advantages to both sides. For example, we might agree to build a system of highways in return for assurances that the Soviet Union would not be allowed to penetrate the country. Bribery is a special case. Here the bargain is with politicians in the underdeveloped country who act from personal interest rather than duty.

*2. Business Friendship.* The aid is given to create or maintain with a government a relationship that is expected to have mutual advantages over a period of time. The aid is, so to speak, a payment on an open account, it being tacitly understood that political advantages will be given in return.

*3. Maintenance of Friendly Governments.* The aid is intended to strengthen and to keep in power a government which is friendly, or at least not unfriendly. This may be done by undertakings, including of course economic development, that will increase the prestige of the recipient government or increase the confidence of its public in it.

*4. Prestige.* The aid is intended to exhibit dramatically the power of the giver and thereby to increase it. As Hobbes said, "Reputation of power is power, because it draweth with it the adherence of those that need protection."

*5. Good Will.* The aid is intended to make the recipient feel well disposed toward the giver and to put him under an implied obligation to return kindness for kindness. Governments are seldom thought to be moved by sentiments such as gratitude, but it is sometimes thought that public opinion may be so moved and that this may have some effect on the policy of governments.

*6. Moral Force.* The aid is expected to affect public opinion by exerting moral force. The giver expects that the nobility of his action will inspire the recipient to act upon equally high moral principles.

Those who write about aid tend to rank these methods on an ascending scale of moral worth. David Lilienthal, for example, deplores the spectacle of "the representatives of a noble nation up to their elbows in the cynical international bazaar, there to bargain and haggle and make deals by which we trade our money or credit or technical aid for 'friendship'"; aid, he says, "should provide a demonstration of the kind of people our system of political and economic freedom is capable of producing."[13] It is hard to understand these judgments. If a government is willing to trade favors in foreign policy for material assistance, why should it or the country with which it trades be criticized? The expression "friendly governments" means, Aristotle remarked, not governments that love each other but ones that exchange favors. A trade, moreover, is the outcome of free action by the governments involved; one government does not manipulate the other in the sense of using the other without the other's knowledge or consent. Efforts to exercise influence by "good will" or "moral force," on the other hand, *do* involve manipulation. One who is placed under a diffuse obligation by the receipt of a favor is obviously less free than one who has made a definite exchange in a bargaining process.

From the standpoint both of morality and American national interest we ought to prefer to give aid on a *quid pro quo* basis. The possibilities of doing this, however, are extremely limited. Most of the underdeveloped countries are pathologically sensitive about "honor" and accordingly will not tolerate any suggestion that we should get something for our money. The few governments which will sell favors are reactionary ones which cannot long survive. Doing business with these may be necessary, but will probably make it harder for us to get on a satisfactory basis with those that will replace them. The *quid pro quo* principle is therefore not one which can be relied upon very far or very long.

To use aid to increase American prestige is foolish. Our power, military and economic, is not doubted anywhere. The trouble is that those who appreciate our power are nevertheless in a position to ignore it because they know that we cannot or will not use it. Cuba is a case in point. Reminders of our power will not change the situation.

"Good will" and "moral force" can make an effect only by working upon public opinion in the recipient countries and not by influencing governments directly. But "public opinion" may accept American aid—conceivably even accept it gratefully—without viewing our foreign policy in a more favorable light. Moreover, in the countries in question, a favorable public opinion would not mean any change of government policy. In the under-

[13] "Needed: A New Credo for Foreign Aid," *New York Times Magazine*, June 26, 1960.

developed countries, public opinion does not include the opinion of the masses of people, most of whom are peasants. The only opinion that counts is that of the small ruling elites. These elites will not be grateful to us and will not respect us for saving peasants from starvation. Although they are largely Western-educated, they do not entirely share our moral standards. What we think is noble, they may think merely foolish. The very idea of public-spiritedness is unintelligible to educated people in most parts of the world, including some that share the Judaeo-Christian tradition.

The effect of aid upon opinion in the underdeveloped countries is at least as likely to be unfavorable as to be favorable. Having to feel grateful is not a pleasant position to be in; it implies inferiority. The underdeveloped countries, precisely because their inferiority is already so obvious, will be made more hostile by every reminder of it.

THE ALTERNATIVE OF NO AID

However dim the prospects of improving our security by the methods of indirect or of direct aid, these methods—either or both—would nevertheless have to be relied upon if it could be shown that the alternative is likely to be national disaster. Criticism of aid must therefore consider, if only very briefly, the alternative of no aid at all.

If the United States were to follow such a policy, the worst that could happen is that the underdeveloped countries would all fall to the Communists and be organized by them into an aggressive military and economic alliance to bring about our destruction.  There are tremendous military advantages to us in having military missile bases, tracking stations, and other installations in some parts of the underdeveloped world (not, however, in Africa south of the Sahara, India, or Latin America) and, to a lesser extent, in not having Soviet installations close to us. Valuable as they are, however, our survival as a nation probably does not depend upon these installations. It depends upon our nuclear deterrent, and this would be about the same (although more costly) if instead of having bases abroad we had more and larger missiles within our borders and on our submarines.

The economic disadvantages of withdrawal from the underdeveloped countries would be far less serious than the military ones. Economists say that if all of our trade with the underdeveloped areas ceased, our national income would not stop rising, although it might rise somewhat more slowly than otherwise. It is even arguable that "no aid and no trade" would leave us better off than "aid and trade."

The cultural losses that we would suffer by withdrawal can also easily be overestimated. The contribution of the underdeveloped countries to the enrichment of our culture has been small, and will certainly remain so for a long time to come.

It is often said that the United States could not long stand isolated in a totalitarian world: our confidence in our institutions and traditions and our respect for freedom would, it is said, sooner or later give way under the strenuous propaganda that would stream from all directions. This supposition is plausible, but so also is the contrary supposition. Our response to Hitler and, thus far, to the Soviets has been to extend and reaffirm our faith in democracy, and there is no reason to expect a change. Withdrawal from the underdeveloped areas might indeed give aid and comfort to paranoid and native-Fascist elements in the United States. But if the withdrawal were justified on reasonable and humanitarian grounds, as the least among evils, and if it were supported by the majority of decent and well-intentioned people, its political significance could afford the native Fascists no satisfaction at all.

The real danger to our morale and institutions would come not from a calculated withdrawal but from being pushed from one country after another after having lavished good will and wealth in futile efforts to remain. A long series of humiliating failures might cause us to lose confidence and self-respect and might lead to recriminations and to loss of trust in each other. If the dynamic of the processes of transition from pre-industrial to industrial society proves such as to make it virtually certain that we will fail politically even if we succeed economically, then it would certainly be better to withdraw with dignity than to be forced out in failure.

The case for withdrawal depends, it should be noted, upon the assumption that conditions will arise to make the alternative of not withdrawing relatively undesirable. In other words, withdrawal is not good in itself. It would be far better for us to maintain a close association with the underdeveloped areas if we could do so at a cost (not alone in money, of course) not unreasonably high in relation to the advantages to be derived from the association.

This is the worst that can happen if we give no aid. It is not likely to happen, however. Neither the Soviets nor any other country could, even if we withdrew from the underdeveloped parts of the world, organize all or even most of it into a cohesive bloc. (This is not to say, of course, that the Soviets, the Chinese, or others might not take possession of some countries and exercise much direct or indirect influence in others.) The Soviets are no more able than we to command the tides of nationalism; even among the presently Communist countries there are differences of interest and ideology that prevent concerted action. What is more, the Soviets cannot bring about the economic development of the underdeveloped countries for the same reasons, among others, that we cannot bring it about; and in the unlikely event that they should try, they will probably make themselves hated, just as we will probably make ourselves hated if we persist in trying. If it were possible for us to bestow the underdeveloped areas upon them it might well be to our advantage to do so in order that they might suffer the expense and incur the hatred that will otherwise be ours.

## II. Other Ultimate Justifications

We turn now to a consideration of the doctrines justifying aid on grounds other than its contribution to national security.

### Altruism as a Basis for Aid

Some say that we ought to extend aid for humanitarian reasons even if there is no possibility of any advantage to us from doing so. Two major objections may be made to this doctrine. One is that "doing good" may be impossible because we do not know even in general terms what it consists of for another culture; because, even if we do know what it consists of in general, we do not know what it consists of concretely in the particular circumstances of time and place; or because, even if we know what it consists of concretely, we cannot bring about the effects we intend, or can bring them about only at the risk of bringing about other, unintended effects which will make the situation worse on the

23

whole than before. Doing good cannot be equated to obvious physical improvements like better diet. It must be relative to some conception of the good life and the good society or, rather, of the best life and the best society possible under the circumstances. Are we in a position to judge for other cultures what is best absolutely or best under the circumstances? Assuming for purposes of argument that the answer to both questions is "Yes," do we know how to proceed? Will we be doing good, if, for example, we prevent starvation without at the same time reducing the rate of population increase, and thus lower average incomes and perhaps thereby prevent the occurrence of radical adjustments without which there is no possibility of sustained economic growth? Will we be doing good if we set in motion a process which leads to totalitarian repression in the manner of the Chinese?

If we try to improve matters and fail, perhaps thereby making people worse off, that our intentions were good will not in the least lessen the suffering we will have caused. From our point of view, the goodness of our intention is very important. But from the point of view of the peoples being acted upon, it is not what we want to achieve but what we are likely to achieve that is important.

The other major objection that may be made to the doctrine of altruism is that our political philosophy does not give our government any right to do good for foreigners. Since the seventeenth century, Western political thought has maintained that government may use force or the threat of force to take the property of some and give it to others only if doing so somehow serves the common good, meaning, of course, the good of those from whom the property is taken as well as the good of those to whom it is given. Those who do not belong to a given political community—that is, those who are not its citizens—cannot, under this theory, be given, *for purely altruistic reasons*, the property of those who do belong to it; such giving could not, by definition, serve the common good of the community. In short, government may take from citizens and give to foreigners when doing so serves the common good of the citizens, but it may not do so if (as the doctrine of altruism assumes) all advantage will accrue to foreigners and none to citizens.

That aid cannot be justified under the federal Constitution unless some national interest will be served by it goes without saying. But even our state governments, which we are prone to think can do anything not given to the federal government to do, cannot act except to serve the common good of their peoples.

These considerations may seem legalistic or antiquarian. If Americans wish to do good abroad through the instrumentality of their government they will certainly not be prevented by theoretical considerations. But the theoretical problem must sooner or later be faced, for presumably no American believes that there is no limit whatever to the right of the state to coerce its citizens.

### AID "BECAUSE IT IS RIGHT"

This doctrine asserts that the United States should give aid because the moral law requires doing so. A nation as rich as ours, this doctrine says, sins if it does not sacrifice for the sake of the poor.

Whether the origin of this obligation to be charitable is believed to arise from the will of God or from nature, it is placed upon *persons* and not upon organizational entities like corporations and governments. Aid has moral significance only as it expresses the intention of *persons* as distinguished from *office-holders*. One can imagine a government giving aid without the knowledge or consent of its citizens and perhaps even over their strong opposition. Aid so given would be morally meaningless. One who taxes Peter to give to Paul does not thereby gain moral credit either for himself or for Peter.

Those who advocate aid "because it is right" should favor making it a matter for voluntary contributions. To the extent that a government takes more from some (and less from others) than they would wish to give, it deprives the aid of moral significance.

### AID FOR NATIONAL SELF-IMPROVEMENT

Another ultimate justification for aid is that the giving of it will improve the quality of American life. Millikan and Rostow regard this justification as second only to the promotion of national security in importance. "American society," they say, "is at its best when wrestling with the positive problems of building a better world"; we need "the challenge of world development to keep us from the stagnation of smug prosperity."[14]

---

[14] *A Proposal*, pp. 7 and 8.

Those who take this view seem to have one or another of two kinds of improvement in mind. Some think that drawing the individual into a great, idealistic national endeavor will turn him from the frivolous and demoralizing distractions characteristic of a commercial culture and by so doing will strengthen and deepen his attachment to what may be called collective values. Whether the dangers of commercialism and of individualistic alienation from society are really as great as this assumes and whether, even if they are, foreign aid is a suitable way of dealing with them, will appear extremely doubtful to people whose conception of the good society does not stress the values associated with collective life.

Improvement in our national life, other proponents of aid say, would occur through the strengthening of the impulse to reform and of the institutions through which reformers work, which would be an accompaniment of extensive aid. Just as the atom bomb strengthened the position of scientists and of science in our society, so, it is argued, aid on a vast scale would strengthen those who want to make the society over. This argument, too, cuts both ways: those who do not want to see reformers and reform institutions strengthened will oppose aid if they take the argument seriously.

### III. Democracy and Aid Doctrine

Nothing that has been said constitutes a decisive argument against aid. Reasonable men having the same information and the same general values may well come to opposite policy conclusions. That many thoughtful people favor giving aid does not, then, require any explanation. But that few thoughtful and public-spirited people oppose giving it, or have serious misgivings about it, and that after more than ten years of aid there has been practically no serious discussion of aid doctrines—this *does* require explanation.

The most influential writings about aid doctrine are full of clichés and sweeping statements that turn out on close examination to be meaningless or else entirely unsupported by evidence. Economists who write on aid generally take it for granted that the whole problem is one of raising incomes. Whether this will contribute to the welfare of the recipient peoples, to the peace of the world, or to the security of the United States they rarely seem to consider.

## American Foreign Aid Doctrines

In most of the discussion, the hard choices that must be made are obscured by a fog of moralizing. Moralizing is advocacy, as a basis for action, of principles that do not take into account features of the concrete situation that render them inapplicable or inappropriate. The moralizer averts his gaze from the features of the real situation that constitute the crux of the practical problem, and then, unhampered, tells us how we ought to act in a world that is not the one in which we must act. He warns severely against extending aid to corrupt tyrannies or reactionary ruling oligarchies. This would be good advice if the real choice were between a corrupt tyranny and an honest democracy. Alas, it seldom is, and when it is, his advice is not needed. A genuine problem exists only when the choice must be made between, say, a corrupt tyranny and a Communist one—and in such cases the advice of the moralizer is confusing or pernicious. He, however, refuses to acknowledge the existence of the genuine problem. If it is pointed out to him that supporting a corrupt tyranny may in some circumstances be necessary to avert something worse, he replies blandly that "the proper and the practical courses coincide."[15] If it is pointed out to him that there may be an incompatibility between the security interests of the United States and the development needs of some underdeveloped countries, he assures us that "as long as our policies are designed to help these societies develop in directions which meet the real interests of their own people, our political and our moral interests coincide."[16]

Aid doctrine does not face up to the tragic facts which constitute the problem: that vast areas of the world will probably not achieve a very significant and widespread improvement in levels of living for at least several generations; that they will probably not learn to govern themselves even tolerably well; that such development as occurs is as likely to be inspired by hate as by good will or moral respect; that it may therefore prove to be a disaster for the United States and for all mankind; and that the measures which promise the most present advantage to the West in its struggle for survival are in general the ones that are least

[15] J. K. Galbraith, *The Liberal Hour* (Boston: Houghton Mifflin, 1960), p. 23.
[16] Millikan and Blackmer, *The Emerging Nations*, p. 145.

likely to lead to self-sustained economic growth in the under-developed countries. Instead of looking squarely at these tragic facts and dealing with them politically—instead, that is, of framing courses of action that may not be admirable by absolute standards (and may indeed be downright evil by the standards of the moralizers) but are nevertheless workable and the best that the situation allows of—the writers on aid tell us that if only we are more generous, more enterprising, and more aware of the needs and interests of other cultures, all will be well both for them and for us.

The reason for the unsatisfactory character of discussion—for its optimistic, moralizing, and apolitical tone—is to be found in the nature of the American political system. Our political system works best when "interests" (the concrete and usually material advantages that individuals seek for themselves) rather than "principles" (general ideas about what would be good for the society) are at stake. When interests clash, the interested parties are highly motivated to make the strongest possible case for what they want and to find weaknesses and loopholes in the arguments of their opponents. This competition usually results in a thorough scrutiny of every aspect of the issue. By the same token, when the interested parties are all on the same side of the question or when the matter is decided on the basis of principle rather than interest, the system is likely to work in a slipshod way, few pros and cons being pressed because no one has as much incentive to press them. This has been the situation with regard to aid. The parties most keenly interested in it (farmers and manufacturers wanting subsidized markets) have been in favor of it; opposition has been mainly on grounds of principle.

For another thing, it is in the nature of our political system to bring to the fore issues which the President can use to generate a public opinion that will support him. Presidents have always had to find ways of overcoming by informal means the extreme decentralization of formal authority—the checks and balances and divided powers—so skillfully contrived by the Founding Fathers. Party loyalty, patronage, and logrolling are among the ways this has been done. Today voters and politicians are more than ever concerned with political principle and therefore the old devices for overcoming the decentralization of authority no longer suffice and must be supplemented by others. As Sir Henry Sumner

Maine observed three-quarters of a century ago, to Party and Corruption, the influences which have hitherto shown themselves capable of bringing a large number of men into civil discipline, democracy has added a third: "generalization, the trick of rapidly framing, and confidently uttering, general propositions on political subjects."[17] Foreign aid is a subject (space exploration seems to be another) that is extremely serviceable in creating the "levity of assent" required nowadays to strengthen the power of the Executive.

There are doubtless several reasons why it is so serviceable. The most important, perhaps, is that it appeals to a millennial tendency in the American mind. Americans, as Kenneth W. Thompson has pointed out, have always abhorred force, distrusted diplomacy, and put their faith in comprehensive formulas for solving the world's problems. Confident that they can regenerate the world without resort to force, they have advanced one millennial idea after another; foreign aid is for the present decade what the United Nations was for the last one and what arbitration and the World Court were for the 1920's.

Our political system has brought this millennial tendency constantly to the fore. It has done so in part by preventing the formation of an elite of statesmen who might have a considerable leeway to decide matters on the basis of a professional view. Our statesmen have instead been mostly amateurs who shared the popular ideals and myths. The system has also given importance to the millennial tendency by admitting the general public to an extraordinarily close participation in the making of foreign policy and in its day-to-day conduct.

Americans are apt to feel that they should participate in the making of foreign policy just as they should in the making of, say, farm policy. There is great danger in this. It arises because *goodness*, morality in ordinary personal relations (e.g., kindness, sympathy, liberality, and the desire to see justice done), is sometimes incompatible with *virtue*, morality in matters of state. Private persons ought to act on the principles of goodness, but rulers—those who have accepted responsibility for protecting a society from its enemies —do not have the right to enjoy the luxury of goodness when goodness might endanger the society. They must do what the welfare

[17] *Popular Government* (New York: Henry Holt, 1886), pp. 107 and 108.

of their society demands (that is, they must act virtuously) even though this may require of them actions which, by the standards of ordinary personal relations, are unjust or without kindness. As Churchill has written, "The Sermon on the Mount is the last word in Christian ethics. Everyone respects the Quakers. Still, it is not on these terms that Ministers assume their responsibilities of guiding states."[18]

It *is* on these terms, however, that public opinion guides states. So far as it acts morally, a public acts from goodness, not virtue. It may, of course, act amorally or immorally, as, for example, when it is self-deceived or in a fit of passion. But it cannot calmly and reflectively decide to violate its own fundamental principles and to profane what it holds sacred. It is hard even for the experienced statesman to acknowledge to himself the occasional necessity of subordinating goodness to virtue (that is, of doing what by the standards of ordinary personal relations is evil in order to secure the public welfare); for a whole people to see and accept this necessity is beyond the bounds of possibility. And even if it were possible, it would lead to the eventual disintegration of the society, for once the principles of goodness had been publicly challenged and found unacceptable as criteria by which to decide a great public question, their authority in the ordinary relations of private life would be weakened or destroyed. When, therefore, consideration must be given to transgressing the moral principles of a society, the considering must be done by an elite set apart for the purpose—one which, like a bomb decontamination squad, having special skills that fit it for its task, is willing to endanger itself for the sake of the society. Professional statesmen—those of them who know their job and do it—belong to such an elite.

The goodness of democracy, or, more precisely, the subordination of virtue to goodness that occurs when public opinion enters into the making and the execution of policy, is particularly dangerous in foreign relations. The inveterate goodness of American public opinion accounts to a large extent not only for the deficiencies in our national discussion about aid doctrines but also for the general atmosphere of all such discussions, an atmosphere marked by millennial fervor; unreasoning confidence that right, reason,

[18] Winston S. Churchill, *The Gathering Storm* (Boston: Houghton Mifflin, 1948), p. 320.

and democracy will eventually prevail; abhorrence of force even in the best of causes; profound distrust of diplomacy, of bargaining, and of self-interest; and naive confidence in the efficacy of good examples, noble sentiments, and benevolence as means of exerting influence.

These distortions in our national view of things are likely to cause us to do great injury to ourselves and to others. But if the analysis here is correct, there is nothing that can be done to change the situation fundamentally. Warning the public that its goodness will lead to disaster can have no effect. For the public's very goodness will prevent it from seeing the necessity sometimes of putting trust not in goodness but in men capable of doing what the welfare of mankind requires.

# HOLLIS B. CHENERY

•

# OBJECTIVES AND CRITERIA FOR
# FOREIGN ASSISTANCE

Discussions of the rationale of foreign aid are complicated by the fact that there are several accepted reasons for the United States to extend assistance to other countries. Each of these reasons leads to a different set of criteria for determining whether a country should receive aid and how much. Since these several criteria often lead to conflicting conclusions, it is necessary in each case to identify the nature of the United States interest in a particular country before trying to evaluate our aid program.

A second complication in judging aid programs arises from the fact that different types of assistance—loans, development grants, military assistance, and technical cooperation—typically affect more than one of the United States objectives in a country. This fact prevents the making of a clear-cut separation among types of aid according to both their nature and their function and has caused successive Administrations to vary the categories of aid over the years. This change in nomenclature and coverage has added to the confusion as to the fundamental objectives and mechanisms of foreign assistance.

In presenting the Act for International Development to Congress in the spring of 1961, the present Administration made an effort to relate the several categories of aid as clearly as possible to their primary objectives. At the same time, it attempted to shift the emphasis in aid programs from short-term political and military objectives to long-term economic and social objectives. In this context, the conflict among aid criteria frequently becomes even more acute.

The present paper attempts to define the functions of foreign aid as one of the instruments of American foreign policy and to clarify the several objectives and categories of aid. My principal objective is to provide an analytical framework for the discussion and evaluation of aid programs.

## I. AID OBJECTIVES AND INSTRUMENTS

### A. THE OBJECTIVES

In the most general sense, the main objective of foreign assistance, as of many other tools of foreign policy, is to produce a political and economic environment in which the United States can best pursue its own social goals. The long-term economic and social progress of other countries can be regarded either as a prerequisite for the kind of international community that we need for our own selfish interest or as an end in itself. In either case, we should be concerned to promote rising levels of income, modernization of economies, independent political systems, and other features of societies that satisfy their own citizens as well as the international community.

The second objective, which concerns the immediate future, is internal stability, which is sought by giving financial support in times of economic crisis, by preventing internal disorders, and by other measures that help existing governments to stay in power. The measures taken to preserve economic and political stability may or may not also promote long-term economic and social development. The conflict is acute when the existing government is not development-oriented and a change might be more conducive to growth.

The third major objective of foreign assistance is security of the United States and its allies from external aggression. This objective is sought directly by the provision of armaments, the securing of military bases, and where critically important, the preclusion of Soviet-bloc penetration. External security is both a short-term and a long-term objective. It is supported in the long run by the economic development of the United States and its allies and in the short run by the maintenance of political stability.

While recognizing the interrelationships among these three objectives, we should keep them separate because the measures taken to achieve them vary in their impact and sometimes one must be sacrificed to another.

33

# Hollis B. Chenery

The categories of aid that are incorporated in present and past legislation represent a compromise among three types of classification:

(*a*) *By method of financing:* hard loans, loans under easier terms, sales for local currency, grants.

(*b*) *By objective:* long-term development, political and economic stability, maintenance of military forces.

(*c*) *By type of resource transferred:* agricultural commodities, machinery and equipment, other commodities, personnel.

The principal categories of aid now used may be summarily described in terms of these three principles of classification as:

*1. Development Grants.* The provision of (*a*) grants for (*b*) development purposes. The resources transferred are to a large extent personnel. The main focus is on education, broadly defined. Capital goods and commodities related to technical assistance projects are also included.[1]

*2. Development Loans.* The provision of (*a*) loans repayable in dollars for (*b*) long-term development purposes. Any type of resource may be transferred, but the main components are machinery and equipment (for project loans) and other commodities (for non-project or program loans).

*3. Supporting Assistance.* The provision of (*a*) grants or loans for (*b*) immediate political and economic stability and to offset the effects of military expenditures. The resources transferred may be any sort of commodity.

*4. Military Assistance.* The provision of (*a*) grants, loans, or sales of (*c*) military supplies and equipment and training services. The principal objective (*b*) is external security, but internal stability is an aim of increasing importance in some countries.

*5. Food for Peace.* The provision of (*a*) grants, loans, or sales for local currency of (*c*) surplus agricultural commodities. The objectives may be in any of the three categories.

---

[1] This category therefore includes the narrower category of technical assistance as well as related activities that were previously covered from one of the categories of commodity aid.

## Objectives and Criteria for Foreign Assistance

The principal change from categories used in previous years has been the effort to identify more clearly the purpose for which aid is given. The former categories of Defense Support and Special Assistance have therefore been abandoned in an effort to focus more sharply on the development objective and to distinguish development aid from the amounts still needed for short-term political and economic objectives. The classification by purpose breaks down in the case of agricultural commodities, however, because this form of aid makes use of a particular kind of resource which is in surplus supply in the United States, primarily because of political resistance to carrying out economic adjustments in our productive structure. The amounts of aid that can be given under the Food for Peace program are limited by the nature of local demand and supply in each country, but in countries that can absorb them under our "normal marketing" rules the additional resources provided in this way can be used for any of the three purposes of other types of assistance.

### C. RELATIONS OF OBJECTIVES TO INSTRUMENTS

To gauge the effect of foreign aid, we must look at the changes that a country makes in its total use of resources rather than just at what it does with our assistance. For example, if country X receives a development loan of $50 million for a steel mill and at the same time shifts $50 million of its own resources to its defense budget, the net effect of the loan is to finance an increase in military expenditure. The opposite may equally well be true. By financing imports of military equipment, we may enable a country to devote a higher proportion of its own foreign exchange and budget resources to developmental purposes. Since we usually relate our assistance to projects which both the United States and the recipient regard as having high priority, the added resources are likely to free some existing funds for use elsewhere. Therefore, the marginal increment in resource use does not in general correspond very closely to the type of aid provided. It is only when the expenditure desired by the United States is one that the country itself will forgo entirely in the absence of aid that the direct use of aid can be equated to the net effect on the economy.

The logical conclusions of the preceding argument are that (a) the donor of aid will have little or no control of the net impact of aid on the recipient unless he examines and influences the total proposed use of resources; and (b) the form of aid is largely immaterial to the receiving country so long as the proposed uses are known in advance and are within its own priorities for total resource use.

These conclusions apply with greatest force to well-organized governments which are able to allocate the total resources available to them without regard for the source. This was the case of England and other northern European countries in the Marshall Plan period, cases in which attribution of United States assistance to particular projects or commodities was largely a formality. It is also largely true of Yugoslavia, India, Israel, and a small number of other less developed countries which have well-defined priorities that are not much affected by the form that assistance from the United States and other foreign donors takes. In most underdeveloped countries, however, the offer of a particular kind of aid will have some effect on total resource use, either because the government does not have clear priorities of its own or because it does not have sufficient flexibility in shifting its other resources from one use to another.

## II. CRITERIA FOR AID

The use of foreign assistance as an instrument of United States policy requires judgment on the following questions:

(i) The probable effect of aid on the economy, military strength, and social structure of each recipient country.

(ii) As among countries, the relative importance to the United States of achieving the predicted results in each.

(iii) Alternative ways of achieving the same objectives.

(iv) The value received from additional foreign aid as compared to the value placed on alternative uses of United States budgetary funds.

A better judgment on these questions can be reached by considering alternative means of reaching given objectives and by reducing comparisons to quantitative terms whenever this is feasible. For purposes of discussion, I shall first treat the several objectives of foreign aid as separable and consider the problem of allocating aid resources to achieve each of them.

## Objectives and Criteria for Foreign Assistance

The nature of the simplification that is introduced into the over-all allocation problem by this analytical procedure is as follows. For each of the three objectives of aid—external security, internal stability, and economic and social development—we can specify either a given set of requirements (targets) or a given amount of available resources. By either device the total problem is divided into three parts. Each of these suballocation problems may then be stated as either: (*a*) to achieve the given requirements with minimum cost to the United States or (*b*) to achieve maximum progress toward the given objective from the fixed resources tentatively assigned to this use.

To resolve the over-all allocation problem, we can combine these two alternatives in various ways. One combination which corresponds reasonably well to the present philosophy of United States assistance is to fix minimum acceptable expenditures for the military security and internal stability objectives and then to maximize long-term social development of the less developed countries subject to these short-term limitations. Once a tentative set of aid programs is arrived at in this way, the balance among the several objectives must be re-examined, as indicated in Section III.

### A. AID FOR ECONOMIC AND SOCIAL DEVELOPMENT

Among the three general objectives, the rationale of aid for economic and social development is perhaps the clearest. Assume that the problem is to allocate a given sum among a number of countries so as to produce a pattern of social development that is in the best interest of the United States.

We can distinguish three links between the input of United States aid and the outcome of desired social development:

(i) The effectiveness of aid in producing economic growth, as measured by the increase in national income and desirable changes in the economic structure.

(ii) The social changes that are likely to accompany (and be permitted by) economic improvement.

(iii) The importance to the United States of economic and social progress in the given country.

The economist's approach to this problem is to divide it into two parts: a *productivity aspect*, describing the first relation between aid and economic growth, and a *valuation aspect*, expressing the relative importance attached to the kind of social change that is expected to accompany economic growth. If we could give a numerical value to the social change produced in each country, it would be possible (conceptually, at least) to allocate aid among countries so as to produce a maximum return for a given amount of United States resources.[2] Even in the absence of such measurements, this approach permits us to separate *productivity criteria* and *valuation criteria* in a useful way.

The criteria that received most attention in the presentation of foreign assistance legislation to Congress in 1961 were the productivity criteria. The best single measure of the productivity of aid is the amount of increase in the national product that is achievable from a given amount of aid over a given period of time. The following elements affect this productivity ratio:

(*a*) The country's endowment of natural resources.

(*b*) The foreign exchange earnings of the country and its need for imported goods. (Aid may have a very high productivity when there is a structural deficit in the balance of payments that takes several years to eliminate.)

(*c*) The total increase in skilled manpower that will result from the capital and technical assistance provided.

(*d*) The increase in total investment resources, including tax collections, that will take place as a result of the increase in incomes.

(*e*) The over-all efficiency of resource use in the country. In countries in which most of these factors are favorable, such as Japan, Israel, or Yugoslavia, the increase in total output per dollar of aid given may be very high because of the complementary nature of the external resources and the domestic resources that can be mobilized. In less favorable cases, such as Laos or Haiti, there may be little mobilization of local resources as a result of aid, and a very low productivity ratio.

The elements in the valuation criterion are more difficult to specify with any precision. In general terms, our long-term social objective is to produce independent societies that are capable of self-sustaining economic and political evolution. The value

[2] This approach is developed by Charles Wolf in *Foreign Aid: Theory and Practice in Southern Asia* (Princeton: Princeton University Press, 1960).

that should be given to democratic forms (with perhaps less political stability) as compared to more central authority (with perhaps greater stability and economic growth) is a question that can at best be answered only for particular countries in the light of all the circumstances.

Two aspects of the development process are important to the making of intercountry valuations. The first is that a significant minimum change must be made in the social and economic structure of most underdeveloped countries in order to secure continued progress. An even spreading of United States assistance will therefore be less effective than a concentration which provides at least this minimum change in the more promising countries. Second, there is a point beyond which the need for external aid diminishes, as countries become more able to provide their own resources for growth.

In the past ten years, several less developed countries which formerly received substantial amounts of United States assistance have reached the point where they no longer require our aid for their continued growth. Included in this group are Italy, Japan, and Yugoslavia.[3] In these cases, the productivity of additional aid would be as high as or higher than that of most countries to which we give assistance. Notwithstanding this fact, aid to these countries has been greatly reduced or eliminated because they can now finance their own continued development. At the other extreme are countries that receive relatively little aid for opposite reasons: a low productivity of aid, despite a high valuation of the desirability of economic and social progress. In this second category, it is low absorptive capacity that limits the aid extended.

### B. AID FOR POLITICAL STABILITY

Economic assistance is one of the instruments of foreign policy that are used to prevent political and economic conditions from deteriorating in countries where we wish to sustain the present government. As with development aid, the analysis of this assistance can be broken down into a productivity aspect and a valua-

---

[3] Several other countries, such as Greece, Israel, and Taiwan, would be in this category if they did not have such heavy defense burdens.

tion aspect. The productivity of aid for stabilization depends in part on the nature of the government's economic difficulties and the extent to which they can be relieved by additional imports. The extent to which a government's political difficulties stem from the economic situation is also an important element.

A central question concerning this use of aid is the perverse incentive effect which it may have on governments that do not use their resources efficiently. Frequently, the availability of foreign help merely removes the pressure on the government to undertake needed political and economic reforms. Unlike the case of development aid, for which there are some objective measures of success, it is not possible to compare with any accuracy what has happened with aid for political purposes to what would have happened without it. It is a matter of political speculation whether Haiti, Bolivia, Jordan, and Laos, for example, are significantly more stable and progressive for having had substantial American assistance than they would have been with less or none.

The number of countries receiving aid mainly for short-run political reasons is relatively small, and this type of aid constitutes only 10 to 15 per cent of our total economic assistance programs. It is probably the most controversial feature of aid policy, however, and the one on which it is most difficult to form a judgment. Since the valuation aspect tends to dominate the productivity aspect in the decision on political aid, there is a tendency to use economic assistance to meet crises in which it can have relatively little effect unless accompanied by other political and economic measures that may not be forthcoming. The threat of a Communist takeover is the strongest political argument for aid, and it sometimes leads to the use of aid whose productivity is very low indeed. Moreover, the problem is complicated by the fact that the process is not readily reversible; whether the aid helps meet the crisis or not, the argument is often made that any sharp reduction in the aid would in itself create a crisis.

Despite the Congressional dissatisfaction with the Supporting Assistance category of aid and our lack of success in some countries in past attempts, there will continue to be strong pressures to use aid for short-run political purposes. Where we are successful, as we were in Greece when its economy and political structure were threatened by civil war, stabilization is followed by long-term growth, and the former is clearly a prerequisite to the latter.

Even if this outcome could only be achieved in one country out of three, it would probably be well worth while. We must, however, accept the greater risks of failure that are inherent in this type of enterprise and not judge the immediate outcome in predominantly economic terms. Above all, we should not allow the fact that the importance of political stability sometimes leads us to undertake risky ventures in low-productivity countries to weaken or obscure the productivity criteria that we seek to apply to the great bulk of our economic aid. We should also resist the temptation to use aid in situations where it can have little effect, no matter how important the objective.

#### C. AID FOR EXTERNAL SECURITY

The preservation of the external security of the United States and its allies is probably the least controversial of the objectives of foreign assistance. Aid for this purpose is provided in the form of military goods and services under the Military Assistance Program. Additionally, the economic impact of military expenditure is also offset to some extent by the provision of nonmilitary commodities under Supporting Assistance and Food for Peace. Since the European countries have become able to take over almost all of their own defense costs, this type of aid now goes mainly to countries in the Middle and Far East. Correspondingly, the share of MAP in total aid has declined since 1954 from over 90 per cent to less than 40 per cent of total assistance, as shown in the following table.

The criteria for allocating military aid by country are in principle quite similar to the criteria for allocating development aid. The productivity aspect is measured by the increased defense effort that the recipient country is prepared to make in return for a given amount of assistance. The value to the United States of additional military strength varies greatly from country to country, however. As in the case of other types of aid, the valuation placed on an additional military effort in a certain country may be so high as to offset the low efficiency with which aid is used. Here again, neither the productivity test nor the valuation test can be used by itself.

One of the main problems in allocating aid for external security is to adjust our policy to changes in military technology and in the strategy of the cold war. In some countries, the threat

U.S. ECONOMIC AND MILITARY AID SINCE 1949 BY BASIC PURPOSE
($ Billions)

| Year | Total U.S. Economic and Military Aid[a] | Rehabilitation of Europe and Other War Damaged Areas[b] | | Military Security[c] | | Stability and Long-Term Development[d] | |
|---|---|---|---|---|---|---|---|
| | | Amount | % of Total | Amount | % of Total | Amount | % of Total |
| 1949 | $8.4 | $7.6 | 90% | $ .7 | 9% | $ .1 | 1% |
| 1950 | 5.2 | 4.8 | 82 | .1 | 2 | .3 | 6 |
| 1951 | 4.6 | 3.0 | 65 | 1.2 | 26 | .4 | 9 |
| 1952 | 3.9 | 1.7 | 43 | 1.9 | 49 | .3 | 8 |
| 1953 | 6.9 | — | — | 6.2 | 90 | .7 | 10 |
| 1954 | 5.8 | — | — | 5.5 | 95 | .3 | 5 |
| 1955 | 5.2 | — | — | 3.8 | 73 | 1.4 | 27 |
| 1956 | 5.7 | — | — | 4.3 | 75 | 1.4 | 25 |
| 1957 | 5.5 | — | — | 3.3 | 60 | 2.2 | 40 |
| 1958 | 5.4 | — | — | 3.3 | 61 | 2.1 | 39 |
| 1959 | 5.8 | — | — | 3.0 | 52 | 2.8 | 48 |
| 1960 | 5.3 | — | — | 2.7 | 51 | 2.6 | 49 |
| 1961 | 6.0 | — | — | 2.2 | 37 | 3.8 | 63 |
| 1962 | 6.9 | — | — | 2.3 | 33 | 4.6 | 67 |
| Total[a] | $82.9 | $17.1 | 20% | $42.9 | 52% | $23.0 | 28% |

[a] Military aid figures are deliveries; economic aid figures and cumulative totals are obligations.
[b] Includes Marshall Plan Aid of $13.4 billion, as follows by year: 1949, $5.9 billion; 1950, $3.6 billion; 1951, $2.4 billion; and 1952, $1.5 billion.
[c] Includes Military Assistance, Defense Support and P.L. 480, Section C, "Common Defense" currencies.
[d] Includes Export-Import Bank, other P.L. 480, all non-Defense Support aid, and other U.S. economic programs.

of internal aggression may now be greater while the external threat may be less than when aid programs were initiated. Furthermore, the maintenance of the economic status quo is not sufficient to prevent internal unrest when economic development is taking place in other countries. In the long run, economic and social development are likely to be as important to the preservation of military security as military aid itself.

### III. The Balance Among Objectives

Up to now, I have followed the procedure of breaking down the general United States objective of strengthening the nations of the free world into three more specific objectives: long-term social and economic development, political stability, and external security. In the actual formulation and execution of aid programs, each of these must in turn be translated into sectors of the economy to be strengthened, types of technical assistance to be provided, military missions to be performed, etc. The further we get from the over-all objective, however, the greater the need for comparison of the advantages of each type of program and for periodic re-examination of their total impact on each country.

After twenty years of United States experience with foreign assistance programs, there is now a general feeling that too much attention has been paid to the crises of the moment and not enough emphasis given to long-term improvements in societies. The most serious criticism that can be made of our aid programs is not that there has been occasional inefficiency or corruption in executing them but that their conception has often been too narrow and short-sighted. Somewhat paradoxically, the attempts to improve the efficiency of execution by focusing on particular projects may have contributed to this short-sighted view of the problem by diverting attention from the total use of a country's resources to the small fraction that is arbitrarily chosen for United States financing.

An attempt is now being made to reverse this trend and to provide aid on the basis of long-term development programs rather than merely for isolated projects. India, Pakistan, and Nigeria are the first countries to receive aid on this basis. It is anticipated that over the next several years a number of other countries will develop sufficiently well organized plans so that commitments can be made for their continuing support and aid can be related to the country's total use of resources.

The recognition that long-term development should receive relatively greater emphasis than in the past has implications both for the allocation of aid among regions and countries and for the composition of country programs. Among regions, Latin America and Africa should receive a greater share over the next few years because of this change in emphasis and because a high proportion of aid to these areas goes for long-term development. The main problem is to raise the productivity of aid to countries in these regions by helping them to make better use of their own resources as well as of those that we provide. This is one of the basic objectives of the Alliance for Progress. At the present time, development loans and grants to most countries in Latin America and Africa are limited more by the ability of these countries to use external resources effectively (the productivity test) than by a shortage of funds from the United States and other sources.

In the countries of Asia and the Near East, which have been receiving substantial amounts of assistance for purposes of internal stability and military security, re-examination of the balance among objectives has initiated a change in the composition of the aid programs. The countries along the Iron Curtain that receive the major part of our military assistance—Korea, Formosa, Vietnam, Pakistan, Iran, Turkey, Greece—have been receiving a mixture of military assistance, supporting assistance to offset the budgetary effect of large defense forces, and development aid. It is impossible to say what the net effect of this combination on the military strength and economic growth of each country has been, because it would be necessary to know what the country would have done with its own resources in the absence of aid. In most countries the development effect is probably greater than is indicated by the amount of aid allocated directly to this purpose, because the country would probably have chosen to reduce its development expenditure in the absence of military aid and supporting assistance. In any case, the total aid is of great importance in most of these countries, however it may be divided by type. Since total aid is a large fraction of their developmental and military expenditures, it is particularly necessary to relate

United States assistance to the total use of resources in these countries; the allocation by type of aid is essentially a tactical device.

## IV. CONCLUSIONS

Several conclusions stand out from this brief survey of the objectives of foreign aid and the criteria for deciding how to achieve them.

1. Foreign assistance should be regarded basically as one of the instruments of foreign policy. In deciding whether or not to use it, alternative instruments such as trade policy or the action of international agencies should be considered.

2. A judgment of the desirability and effectiveness of American aid can only be made on the basis of a clear statement of United States objectives in a particular country. Given the multiple objectives of our aid programs, there is no simple principle of allocation that can be used in all cases.

3. Because the different types of aid are substitutes for each other in varying degrees, there is only an approximate relation between the forms of aid and the main objectives. Aid should therefore be related as much as possible to total programs for resource use. This procedure is likely to increase the effectiveness of United States aid significantly as compared to past methods.

4. In order to promote long-term development to a greater extent, it may be necessary to take some risks in regard to the maintenance of existing governments. In the long run, however, support for progressive governments is likely to be a better way of combatting Communism around the world than giving funds on the basis of immediate political and military threats.

# JOHN NUVEEN

●

# SOCIAL AND POLITICAL AID

Foreign aid is probably the most important and most confused issue that faces the American people. For the first time in the history of our republic, we are confronted with an aggressive and powerful nation that is diametrically opposed to our political, social, and economic principles, finds them an obstacle to its own ambitions, and has, therefore, declared its intention to "bury" us. Even though its declared plans for doing so are basically ideological, we are faced with a struggle for survival, a struggle which we call the Cold War. In fighting this war our strategy has been twofold. We have been spending approximately $40 billion a year for military defense and about $4 billion a year for programs variously constituted but generally described as foreign aid.

An interesting evaluation of our strategy was contained in the Statement of the Idea and Purpose of the People-to-People Program, privately organized in 1957, of which President Eisenhower was honorary chairman. It said in part:

> Every dollar we spend for defense, . . . every atom bomb we can build, every plane, every ship, every gun . . . is wholly negative. These are purely and simply a means of buying time, for they are designed only to prevent physical aggression against us. . . . We will not employ them for attack. We use them to hold off potential enemies while peaceful ideas take hold, and people come to friendship and understanding which will make them unnecessary.

If we accept this analysis, then it is obvious that at least 90 per cent of our Cold War strategy has been negative and the only portion which might be positive is 10 per cent. Or to state it another way, 90 per cent military defense, 10 per cent foreign aid offense.

## Social and Political Aid

Although a strategy of defense is undoubtedly necessary, it neither wins games for competitive teams nor maintains nations in a position of world leadership for very long. The vital element in our foreign policy is, therefore, an effective foreign aid strategy.

Foreign policy takes on special importance in the context of present world events, but its dimensions are generally greater than the average citizen appreciates. Since peace is an important goal of foreign policy, the necessity of fighting a war or preparing for a war represents, to a large extent, the failure of our foreign policy. Inasmuch as approximately 80 per cent of our federal budget is required to pay for past wars and prepare for the possibility of a future one, it is apparent that even if our freedom were not at stake, foreign policy has an impact on our fiscal affairs four times that of all our domestic policies put together.

President Kennedy revealed his estimate of the importance of foreign aid when he said, in his "Special Message on Foreign Aid," March 22, 1961: "We are launching a Decade of Development on which will depend substantially the kind of world in which we and our children shall live."

It therefore becomes important to clarify the confusion that exists about foreign aid. This confusion can be illustrated by quotations from two conservative journals. In the July, 1961, issue of *The Freeman*, published by the Foundation for Economic Education, John C. Sparks, a Canton, Ohio, businessman, says:

> Shortly after World War II the government of the United States imposed upon itself the task of saving the world from poverty and illiteracy—thus proposing to stop the progression of communism over the globe. But sixteen years and expenditures of a hundred billion dollars have not accomplished that goal.

The *National Review* carries a weekly column by James Burnham, who wrote a critical discussion, in the April 10, 1962, issue, on "Ideology and Foreign Aid" and concluded:

> Nor has there ever been, from the start of the foreign aid program in 1947, any objective study of what its actual effects have been, either as a whole or in parts.

Without adding other such quotations, it is clear that there are many people who hold the impression that since World War II

47

we have engaged in a giant giveaway program, $90 to $100 billion to save the world from poverty and illiteracy, dreamt up by idealistic do-gooders and lacking practical purpose. The obvious deterioration of United States prestige abroad in the last few years and the failure to win friends seem to support the charge that the whole foreign aid program has been a giant boondoggle. Thus there comes the natural conclusion that if we haven't been able to develop a sound policy in fifteen years, we never will, and we ought to give up the whole idea.

It is the purpose of this paper to attempt to clarify the confusion inherent in the foregoing statement by setting forth and supporting the following facts:

I. Although our first foreign aid program was the Aid to Greece and Turkey in 1947, the popular concept of foreign aid was established by the Marshall Plan, which originated in 1948 as a program of purely economic aid to Europe. The purpose of these programs was clearly understood and they were very successful.

II. The criticism that foreign aid has been a failure, therefore, can be addressed only to the program of aid to underdeveloped countries which started January 1, 1952. Since this date, the amount of money appropriated for the economic development of the underdeveloped countries has been only about $6 billion, not $100 billion.

III. We have been successful with our economic programs to the developed countries of Europe. We have lacked success with such programs in the underdeveloped countries in the rest of the world. This would indicate a failure to understand the fundamental differences between the developed and underdeveloped nations and to develop a policy for dealing with the basic problems of the underdeveloped nations.

IV. While there have been penetrating analyses of the problems of the underdeveloped countries and recommended policies for dealing with these which emphasize the greater need for social and political aid, there has been a failure on the part of the State Department to carry out such policies. This failure may be attributed basically to the failure of the State Department to readjust its organization, personnel, and operations to enable it to discharge effectively the responsibilities of world leadership, instead of merely observing and reporting events on the world scene.

V. In answer to the defeatists who defend the State Department failures or who advocate a policy of withdrawing from world affairs into a position of isolationism on the grounds that there is little or nothing we can do to effect political change, it should be pointed out that we have a few examples, pilot-plant operations, most notably in Puerto Rico, that demonstrate that political change is possible. Nevertheless, in undertaking this task we are pioneering—sailing uncharted seas and facing problems of great complexity and magnitude. Successful solutions will require sympathetic understanding by the American people, a confidence in the greater vitality of their institutions than those of Communism, and a united will to make whatever sacrifices are necessary to succeed.

## I

Our first foreign aid program was the Aid to Greece and Turkey in 1947. Its basic purpose was clear and simple. It was to help Greece put down the guerrilla rebellion which, if successful, would have delivered Greece into the hands of the Communists. It was also to strengthen the military forces in Turkey so as to remove the temptation of a direct external attack by the Communists to bring Turkey into their fold and thus gain control of the outlet to the Black Sea. The effect of our aid to Greece in assisting it to win the guerrilla war and to build a healthy, free-enterprise economy is one of the most spectacular accomplishments that we have had since World War II and can be witnessed by even the casual visitor.

Although Europe did not have a guerrilla rebellion to contend with in 1947, it was obvious that unless something were done to reverse a dangerous trend, Europe might end up behind the Iron Curtain. At each successive election following the end of the war, an increased number of Communist deputies had been elected to the parliaments in the various countries and a mounting number of cities were electing Communist mayors and Communist councils. The people, facing ultimate starvation due to the steadily declining production which resulted from the economic destruction and dislocation of the war, were seeking some alternative to the course they had been pursuing and were turning in desperation to Communism, which was at hand and making glowing promises. General Marshall outlined the problem and proposed a means of dealing with it. In his now famous speech made at the Harvard commencement, June 5, 1947, he said in part:

> ... The town and city industries are not producing adequate goods to exchange with the food-producing farmer. . . . The farmer or the peasant cannot find the goods for sale which he desires to purchase. . . . He, therefore, has withdrawn many fields from crop cultivation and is using them for grazing. . . . Meanwhile people in the cities are short of food and fuel. So the governments are forced to use their foreign money and credits to procure these necessities abroad. This process exhausts funds which are urgently needed for reconstruction. . . . The modern system of the division of labor upon which the exchange of products is based is in danger of breaking down. . . . The remedy lies in breaking the vicious circle and restoring the confidence of the European people in the economic future of their own countries and of Europe as a whole. . . . It is logical that the United States should do whatever it is able to do to assist in the return of normal economic health in the world, without which there can be no political stability and no assured peace. Our policy is directed not against any country or doctrine but against hunger, poverty, desperation, and chaos. *Its purpose should be the revival of a working economy in the world so as to permit the emergence of political and social conditions in which free institutions can exist.* [Italics supplied.]

The effects of our economic aid to Europe have been so impressive and so well publicized that it is hard to believe that there is any informed person who is not aware of them. A remarkable economic recovery was accompanied by the collapse of Communist influence. As a result, great forces are now working toward a political and economic union of Europe which will comprise a very powerful bulwark against Communist aggression.

## II

Any discussion of the failure of foreign aid must start with our program of aid to underdeveloped countries in 1952. In this connection it is important first to clarify the figure of $100 billion which is so frequently cited in newspapers and national publications. It undoubtedly originates with a generous rounding off of a figure that appears in a government report. The Office of

Business Economics, United States Department of Commerce, has been compiling records of "Foreign Grants and Credits" quarterly since July 1, 1940. In the March, 1961, report, "Table I A.—Summary of Major United States Foreign Assistance. . . Postwar Period July 1, 1945, through March 31, 1961," reveals a total of $83,943,000,000. This figure, which is pertinent to our balance of payments, has very little relevance to the sum total of our foreign aid appropriations; furthermore, there is certainly no basis for casually adding another $16 billion.

There is, however, some justification for the confusion. While the name of the above report, which was originally called "Foreign Transactions of the United States Government," has only been changed once, the title of the balance of payments summary table has been changed successively as follows:

1940—"Summary of Foreign Grants and Credits"

1952—"Summary of Foreign Aid (Grants and Credits) War and Postwar"

1954—"Summary of Foreign Aid (Grants and Credits) Post-war"

1960—"Summary of Major United States Foreign Assistance—Postwar"

It is clear from the above that the origin of this statistical report has nothing to do with the present strategic concept of foreign aid to promote the economic development of less developed areas or to "save the world from poverty and illiteracy." Furthermore, the $84 billion of what is now called "foreign assistance" is misleading. This can be revealed by a breakdown by periods.

The question is, how much of this money was spent to save the world from poverty and illiteracy? Obviously the $48 billion of lend-lease which was originally included in the table compilation had no such purpose. It was our contribution, before our actual participation in the war, to the defeat of Hitler. The $16 billion of postwar relief amounted to little more than the cost of cleaning up after World War II and was essential, as we learned from our experience in World War I, to establishing the peace. The $12.5 billion for European recovery went to nations that are highly literate and whose impoverishment, due to the dislocations of the war, had no relation to the kind of deep-seated poverty we know

| Amount | Period | Purpose |
|---|---|---|
| $48,546,000,000 | The War Years (July 1, 1940 to June 30, 1945) | "Almost exclusively lend-lease" (Not included in total since 1954) |
| $16,300,000,000 | Postwar Relief (July 1, 1945 to March 30, 1948) | "To the relief and rehabilitation of countries devastated by war and to the re-establishment of international economic relationships. . . . Credits constituted slightly more than half of this postwar assistance." |
| $11,390,000,000 | European Recovery Program (April 1, 1948 to Dec. 31, 1951) | Replacing working capital and revitalizing the highly developed European economy. Grants, $10,237,000,000; credits, $1,153,000,000. Carry-overs brought the final total to about $12.5 billion. |
| $39,778,000,000 | Mutual Security Programs since Jan. 1, 1952 (ICA Report of Obligations and Commitments) | The name of the agency administering "foreign aid" was changed in 1952 from Economic Cooperation Administration to Mutual Security Agency, reflecting a change in direction from the developed European nations to the less developed nations and a change in emphasis from economic to military aid. |
| $16,475,000,000 | Balance Miscellaneous | Lend-lease carry-over, International Monetary Fund, Export-Import Loans, Civilian Relief in Korea, Public Law 480, etc. |
| $83,943,000,000 | | |

in the underdeveloped nations of the world. Nor is the $16 billion of miscellaneous items germane, as is obvious from its purpose. If we are going to find monies that could have been devoted "to the elimination of poverty and illiteracy," we will have to look at the $39.8 billion expenditure for the Mutual Security program since January 1, 1952.

Mutual Security aid is broken down as between "military" and "economic," but economic aid is not separated to distinguish between economic development and support of military programs. To get a breakdown and to be able to determine how much has been devoted to economic development of the less developed countries, it is necessary to examine the annual appropriations by Congress. This causes some discrepancy in figures.

### MUTUAL SECURITY APPROPRIATIONS
#### (in millions of dollars)

| Fiscal Year | Military Assistance and Defense Support | Total Development Assistance and Loans | Administration Int'l Agencies and Misc. | Total Appropriations |
|---|---|---|---|---|
| 1953 | $ 5,881 | $ 522 | $ 44 | $ 6,447 |
| 1954 | 4,123 | 329 | 79 | 4,531 |
| 1955 | 2,793 | 335 | 124 | 3,252 |
| 1956 | 2,472 | 354 | 459 | 3,285 |
| 1957 | 3,179 | 402 | 185 | 3,766 |
| 1958 | 2,029 | 638 | 101 | 2,768 |
| 1959 | 2,265 | 750 | 283 | 3,298 |
| 1960 | 1,995 | 976 | 254 | 3,225 |
| 1961 | 2,410 | 962 | 350 | 3,722 |
| | $27,147 | $5,268 | $1,879 | $34,294 |

Thus it appears that Mutual Security and Development Loan Fund *appropriations for economic development of the less developed countries in the nine years since the start of the program have amounted to only $5,268,000,000.* To this can be added a small fraction that cannot be readily determined of the $6.1 billion of Public Law 480 farm products disposal other than that used for alleviation of famine, emergency relief, and defense support.

Instead of the $100 billion expenditure so often criticized, we find that a figure of about $6 billion over a period of nine years is more accurate. But the magnitude of our aid is even less impressive than that. It is obviously not so much poverty as the contrast of poverty with riches which is responsible for the dissatisfaction and unrest of have-not peoples which may serve the Communist cause. If we contrast what we have done to raise the standard of living in the rest of the world with what we have done for ourselves, we get a more accurate picture.

During the last nine years for which figures are currently available (1951 to 1959, inclusive) from the Office of Business Economics, Department of Commerce, the gross private domestic investment in the United States was $522,004,000,000, which comprises investment in new construction and producers' durable equipment. What we have given or loaned to the less developed countries, therefore, to help raise their economic level in nine years is only 1 per cent of what we spent to *maintain and expand* our own. Considering that the United States has only 6 per cent of the world's population and that the less developed nations outside the Communist bloc have 50 per cent of the world's population, the amount we have given or invested to raise the economic level of the people in the less developed nations on a per capita basis is ⅛ of 1 per cent of what we have spent on our own development.

This should dispel any illusion that the present level of our foreign aid is bankrupting our own citizens while the previously underfed, underprivileged natives in the underdeveloped countries are, as a result of our largess, becoming fat and prosperous. It should also effectively answer the businessman who trembles in fear of the potential competition we are building up in the underdeveloped countries through government grants and investments. But most of all, it demonstrates that to the extent that it has been our hope through our aid programs to reduce the economic gap between the standards of living in the developed and underdeveloped countries, thereby lessening the dissatisfaction of the have-nots, which makes them susceptible to Communist subversion, we can be completely disillusioned. It is not surprising that we have not stopped the spread of Communism with dollars.

## Social and Political Aid

### III

In its experience with foreign aid, as has been observed, the United States has had remarkable success with its economic programs in the developed countries of Europe and a notable lack of success in the underdeveloped countries in the rest of the world. It is important to analyze the reasons for this. It might be accounted for by the lesser amount we have provided to the underdeveloped countries in proportion to their population. To compare: for the 250 million people in Europe we spent $12.5 billion in three and one-half years, while to assist the billion or more people in the underdeveloped countries, we have spent only $6 billion in nine years. Roughly, this is half as much, over about two and one-half times as long a period, for four times as many people, or a ratio of about one-twentieth. But this is not, in my opinion, the principal reason for our failure in the latter category, or even an important reason. If we had merely increased the amount of our aid, we might have had even less success.

Our basic failure is the failure to understand the simple and very clear distinction between the task we faced in Europe and the task we now face in the underdeveloped countries of the world. Europe had, through many generations of struggle, established the political and social institutions on which modern societies could be constructed, and these were the foundation of the flourishing industrial economies which existed before the war. The Marshall Plan was purely an economic plan to revive the previously developed economies of Europe. It succeeded not only because it was ably conceived and administered but also because in the highly developed states of western Europe there had been healthy economies that could be revived and political and social institutions that could be restored.

When we confront the problem of the underdeveloped nations, we find there have never been healthy economies to revive or free institutions to restore. The political and social foundations must be created, and this is an infinitely more complex and difficult task than we faced in Europe. Supplying guns to an underdeveloped nation may help it to resist Communist aggression, but it may also increase the power of an oppressive government over

55

its own subjects and thus encourage Communist subversion. Supplying guns does not reduce ignorance and superstition or help to build sound political institutions. Likewise, supplying dollars, which may make possible increased production, does not insure that the benefits will be passed on to the majority of the people and result in a better standard of living. In most cases, the benefits of increased production are skimmed off by a small landowning elite who are protected by a conniving and subservient dictatorship which they support.

It should go without saying that we are concerned with the evolution of underdeveloped nations into strong, *free* nations, not strong, *Communist* nations. The differences between freedom and Communism are basically social and political, which is to say that the most important problem we face in the underdeveloped nations is how to encourage the right kind of social and political change. Economic development is necessarily secondary. If it is undertaken other than in the context of a program of building free institutions, it may strengthen a nation that will soon become Communist. In such a case, our aid is not only wasted, it helps our enemy. But for the past nine years we have failed to develop any philosophy, program, or technique for assisting social and political development—call it change, evolution, revolution, or whatever you will.

The task of building a strong, *free* nation in this modern industrial age is the problem of compressing several thousand years of struggle and change, such as preceded the emergence of our Western culture, into one generation. In turn, this involves an understanding of the forces that have shaped human development and a knowledge of all the facets of human history. This is a new and colossal task, without pattern or precedent.

Are not the underdeveloped countries underdeveloped precisely because they have not had the social and political foundations which permit the development of human resources? Is not this the reason for their failure to construct modern industrial societies? And therefore is it not our first task in building a world of human freedom to help these nations to build the proper social and political foundations? Economic aid may provide the mortar or the labor for constructing foundations, but without the foundations, it cannot build a superstructure that will endure. It will be a house built upon sand. Therefore, we can say that foreign aid for the underdeveloped countries, at the outset, must be primarily social and political if it is going to serve its purpose.

We can support this conclusion with one illustration. It is perhaps an accident of history that mostly Englishmen settled in North America while Spain and Portugal colonized South America, but it is no accident that North America has developed an abundant life while South America has languished in poverty and illiteracy. The Pilgrims and other religious and political groups who came to North America risked physical hardship and even survival in order to translate their concepts of individual liberty and responsibility into practical political institutions, while in South America the conquistadors imported the Spanish and Portuguese concepts of a totalitarian government which are not conducive to the development of individual initiative and responsibility, the foundations of economic development.

This contrast was pointed out fifty years ago by James Bryce in his treatise on South America:

> To understand these countries, one must think of them as having, under the rule of the Spanish Crown and the Church, dropped two centuries behind the general march of civilized mankind. When they were finally liberated in 1825, they were practically still in the Seventeenth, while Europe and the United States were in the Nineteenth Century.[1]

This raises two questions: What are the social and political foundations that must be brought about in South America before a modern economic structure can be erected? And how can they be constructed? Many people seem unaware of the fundamental nature of these questions, even though they accept the diagnosis of the social and political ills of the underdeveloped world. They have such faith in foreign aid, because of the miraculous cures that were produced in Europe, that they regard it as a universal nostrum, like Hadacol. Much of the thinking behind the United Nations Technical Assistance programs and the United Nations Special Fund's extensive program of exploration for natural resources is based on the naive assumption that mechanical skills

[1] *South America: Observations and Impressions* (London and New York: Macmillan and Co., 1912), p. 549.

and a handout of capital will immediately convert the discovered raw materials into a higher standard of living.

Rostow and Millikan, in their popular book entitled *A Proposal*, have suggested that the United States and other developed nations assure "to every underdeveloped Free World country that it can secure as much capital as it can use productively," on the theory that while economic development is slow at first, it soon reaches "the take-off"—"a second stage during which the country makes the complex transition to a position where sustained economic growth becomes possible"—thus making further outside aid unnecessary.

Such a theory, it seems to me, completely fails to recognize that the economic "take-off point" may not be as important as what might be called the social and political "take-off point." It fails to recognize the important contribution that was made to our society by the brave bands of political and religious refugees who risked not only physical well-being but survival to establish the principles of a new social order. We can well ask if the significant "take-off" in the United States was not in 1789, when the declaration of social and political principles proclaimed in 1776 was translated into a Constitution of political institutions which supplied the essential foundations for our spectacular economic development, rather than at some arbitrary stage of the rate of increase in capital formation.

Argentina, a country richly endowed with natural resources, achieved an economic take-off many years ago and became not only the richest nation in Latin America, but one of the richer nations (on a per capita basis) in the world. But it never achieved an adequate social and political take-off. For one thing, most of the land in Argentina was divided up among the officers of the Spanish army that killed off the native inhabitants and has continued in the possession of the descendants of these conquerors in *ranchos* containing as many as a million acres. As a result, most of the European immigrants with agricultural skills who went to Argentina in the nineteenth century became peons, while their brothers who went to the United States were able to acquire homestead plots and become independent landowners.

Ultimately, the lack of social progress was exploited by Peron, who rode into political power with the support of the dissatisfied peons and laboring class. He exhausted the capital resources and accumulated surpluses in generous social programs for the workers, with the result that Argentina's economic level has been retrogressing, and today, although Peron has been thrown out, Argentina finds itself economically weak, politically divided, and hence susceptible to Communist infestation.

Cuba received more American private investment in proportion to its size than any other country in South America except Venezuela and accordingly should have been closer to the economic "take-off point," but the take-off never came because Cuba had made very little progress toward a social and political take-off. And this was the dominant fact in its loss to the Free World.

## IV

The necessity for social and political change is not a novel idea. In 1952 the Council on Foreign Relations of New York decided that it should undertake a study of the "political implications of economic development," and chose Dr. Eugene Staley for this assignment. As is its custom, the Council appointed a distinguished study group to assist him.[2] With the benefit of the discussions with this study group and as a result of his own research, Dr. Staley wrote a book, published in 1954 under the sponsorship of the Council on Foreign Relations, entitled *The Future of Underdeveloped Countries*. Two sentences from the introduction suggest the tenor of the background discussions:

> The second major thesis of this book is that economic development of the underdeveloped countries, while a *necessary* condition, is not a *sufficient* condition to insure the growth in those countries of trends favorable to human well-being and to the better world we should like to see. . . .
> It is inconceivable that large-scale economic development, and particularly industrialization, can take place without

[2] This group, which held a series of meetings during 1952, included the following men who are either now in official positions or have previously occupied positions concerned with international economic problems: Percy W. Bidwell, Jonathan B. Bingham, Gordon R. Clapp, Harlan Cleveland; George S. Franklin, Jr., J. Kenneth Galbraith, Robert L. Garner, Arthur J. Goldberg, William L. Holland, Hugh L. Keenleyside, Milo Perkins, Nelson A. Rockefeller, Phillips Talbot, and Howard Tolley.

bringing great changes in the political and social structures of the underdeveloped areas. Political and social change rarely takes place smoothly and easily. It is likely to involve strain, unrest, and perhaps violence.[3]

But the book does more than identify the necessity of social and political change. Some of the paragraph headings give an idea of the scope of the problems as well as suggestions for dealing with them: "Political and Social Requisites"; "Human Resources and the Organizing Factors"; "Agrarian Reform"; "Capital Formation"; "Population Problems"; "Raw Materials and Industrialization"; "The World Environment."

The sponsorship of Dr. Staley's book was such as should have given it important circulation, but apparently authors of subsequent books on foreign aid and economic development, which are legion, have become so absorbed in their own thoughts that they have either not read or have given inadequate regard to earlier treatises on these subjects. The result is that instead of shedding useful light on and adding helpful understanding of a subject of vital importance, they have contributed confusing contradictions. Two such instances are contained among the eleven studies of the foreign aid program which were completed and published in 1957 at the expense of a special committee of the United States Senate. Both studies covered problems related to Dr. Staley's thesis, that is, the necessity for social and political change, but while they expressed opinions in conflict with the thesis, they made no attempt to explain their disagreement. Study No. 1, by the Center for International Studies, Massachusetts Institute of Technology, was entitled "The Objective of U.S. Economic Assistance Programs." In its summary, it repeated the Rostow-Millikan thesis propounded in *A Proposal*, that for a development-assistance program to be effective, it must have assured continuity and sufficient resources to launch a self-sustaining growth, and then added:

> (3) A development program should concentrate on promoting economic growth, not attempt to serve other peripheral objectives.

[3] Published for the Council on Foreign Relations by Harper and Brothers, New York, 1954, p. 4.

It would seem from this that social and political change is regarded as a peripheral objective, contrary to the Staley valuation. Hence it is easy to disregard the important leverage that economic aid provides for aiding social and political change.

Study No. 3, by The University of Chicago, was entitled "The Role of Foreign Aid in the Development of Other Countries." In a section headed "Social, Cultural and Political Change," it expressed the opinion that economic aid was sufficient to bring about the necessary cultural changes, a direct contradiction of Dr. Staley's thesis. It reads:

> In considering how societies change so as to be capable of sustained economic growth, it is noteworthy that all the changes required in the long run do not have to precede the initiation of rapid growth. Economic change, if it is on a large enough scale and meets with enough success, tends to generate the conditions, both economic and cultural, of its own continuance.

It seems to me, as outlined earlier, that all of Latin America, and Argentina in particular, refutes this statement. Certainly adequate capital was available to Latin America from Europe prior to World War I, and many millions of dollars of South American government loans were floated in the United States in the 1920's. But these monies were not spent wisely. They tended to enrich the politicians rather than the people, and hence adequate economic and cultural change did not result. In one way or another, private investments were expropriated and government loans defaulted. Therefore, not only has it become difficult to attract new foreign capital but domestic capital has fled to the safety of Swiss banks.

More recently there has been a study which reveals greater appreciation of the social and political problems of the underdeveloped countries. Sponsored by the Council on Foreign Relations, it is a study on the problems of South America, by Professor Edwin Lieuwen, Chairman of the Department of History at the University of New Mexico. After consultations and research beginning in 1957, he published his findings in 1960 in a book entitled *Arms and Politics in Latin America*. In the concluding chapter, he makes a simple but forceful statement:

The overwhelming problem in Latin America today and for the foreseeable future is the social revolution.

With the advent of the Kennedy administration, an official study was undertaken by The President's Task Force on Foreign Economic Assistance. In their report, "An Act for International Development, A Summary Presentation," published in June, 1961, is the following significant observation:

### Economic Change Will Require Social Change

. . . We must remember that in many parts of the underdeveloped world we are dealing with societies and economies which have remained unchanged for hundreds or even for thousands of years. If these societies and economies are suddenly to become dynamic and progressive, there must be radical changes in the attitudes, motives, and interests, and, in some cases, in the innermost values of great masses of people.

Perhaps the most important development, however, is that President Kennedy, in announcing the Alliance for Progress, has, for the first time, given official recognition to the fact that a successful program for development in South America must be an alliance or partnership in which our contribution is economic and theirs is social and political.

But the progress that has been made by private study groups, official task forces, and the Chief Executive, in recognizing the importance of social and political development, has, unhappily, not been matched in the State Department. Consequently, this important phase of an effective foreign policy is not being implemented, nor is it likely to be implemented, until there are some fundamental changes in the policies and organization of the agency that is responsible for foreign affairs. It will be well to identify some of these.

The impotence of the State Department caused many people to believe that through lax administration it had become infested with Communists, perverts, and misfits. Frantic personnel investigations failed to confirm these beliefs but did much to undermine morale, discourage initiative, and bring about the resignation of many competent men, who refused to face a future of suspicion and persecution.

## Social and Political Aid

I believe that competent observers will testify that the personnel of the State Department is equal, or superior, to that in other government agencies. It may not be adequate for its present responsibilities, but upgrading personnel will not overcome the justified criticism of the department. Under civil service and other regulations designed to support the so-called merit system, measures have been established in personnel administration to prevent changes with each swing of the political pendulum, but these regulations also inhibit changes dictated by changed conditions and responsibilities.

No department of the government has experienced as revolutionary a change in its responsibilities as has the State Department since World War II. The position of the United States has changed from that of a spectator of the international scene to that of leader in world affairs, as Great Britain has stepped down from world leadership, her mantle falling on our shoulders. The role of the officials manning our far-flung diplomatic posts has changed from one of observing and reporting to one of active leadership. The two roles are as different as those of the sportscaster sitting in the football stand describing the game to his radio listeners and the quarterback on the field calling the signals and carrying the ball.

It is not too difficult to outline the changed world situation and what it demands of our leadership and also to suggest some changes that would make the State Department more effective in implementing that leadership.

The focus of the Cold War is on the underdeveloped nations, who comprise about half of the world's population. To win their allegiance is to defeat the Communists in their struggle for world domination. The underprivileged masses in these countries are determined to achieve a better way of life. Most of them have already thrown off the chains of colonialism and now face the fetters of their own social and political institutions and inadequate leadership.

Our task is to provide the kind of leadership in the processes of change which will produce not only economic development but also independence and freedom as opposed to Communist dictatorship. It might be easier to accomplish this task if we had domination over substantial colonial areas of the world or the

63

opportunity to use our military power directly to bring about quick and positive results, two means by which Great Britain exercised world leadership. We are limited, however, to subtler tools and weapons—persuasion, propaganda, education, and the leverage of economic trade and aid. The use of these requires great skill and should be entrusted only to men of broad experience, demonstrated capacity for leadership, and deep human understanding. Such is not likely to be the case if ambassadorial appointments are made in return for campaign contributions or political favors, or as routine promotions of career officers.

Assuming competent leadership, however, we must recognize the organizational changes that are necessary to permit it to function effectively. The most important single factor in exercising leadership is the influence that our principal representative can have on the leadership of the country to which he is assigned. He must be able to command the respect of those leaders by, among other things, his knowledge of the history, traditions, and problems of their country. This respect will, in some measure, be in direct proportion to the time that he has spent in the country. It will also be influenced by the amount of respect which his own government has for him, as evidenced by the amount of authority which has been delegated to him. Making these observations, we must face the depressing reality of the fact that the average tenure of our ambassadors on their posts in the past several years has rarely exceeded two years and that in the last published *Foreign Service List* (April, 1963) the average tenure of our principal representative in the 105 countries where we have embassies was only 1.64 years. The policy of rotating personnel, which was exacerbated by the recommendations of the Wriston Committee, may have insured objective reporting when we were merely observers of the world scene, but today it insures that our representatives in most countries will not have either the knowledge of local conditions or the confidence of local leaders which are prerequisites for effective influence.

Likewise, a highly centralized organization may have been suitable for collecting and correlating reports on world events, but it is totally unsuited to discharging the responsibilities of leadership in over one hundred countries around the world, which involve formulating policy, revising it from day to day, and translating it into effective action. The unmanageable size and the diffusion of responsibility in a central organization that is trying to run the world account for its ineffectiveness. The incomplete knowledge of the Washington bureaucracy and its lack of confidence in the local negotiators often produce procrastination and evasion on many important issues. A specific example will illustrate this.

A cable recommending a certain policy or action in Greece ultimately reaches the Greek Desk in the State Department, which is manned by an underling. Immediately above him is the Director of the Office of Greek, Turkish, and Iranian Affairs, who is in turn responsible to the Assistant Secretary of State in Charge of the Bureau of Near Eastern and South Asian Affairs. Above him are two Deputy Under-Secretaries of State, one for Political Affairs and one for Administration; then the Under-Secretary of State; and finally the Secretary of State, whose name is signed to the cable which goes back to Greece answering the request for guidance. All these share the responsibility for any action that is authorized. Since at each level above the country desk the officer has a greater work load than the one below him, the issue receives less and less consideration as it moves higher in the organizational echelons.

It is high time that the State Department adopted some of the principles of administrative management, including decentralized authority, that have been developed by our business enterprises in handling their far-flung operations. This can be done without any lessened emphasis on the need for consistent and co-ordinated international policy.

It appears obvious from the several unsuccessful attempts to revitalize the State Department in the past dozen years that the kind of revolutionary reorganization that is needed can never come from within. It will have to be imposed by a strong Chief Executive who can enlist the understanding and support of Congress. It can be done in one of two ways: either by declaring a moratorium on present civil service and foreign service regulations, or by starting a new Department of Foreign Affairs and transferring to it the functions that concern the exercise of our world leadership. The latter, a course recommended in the Brookings Institution report of 1959 to the Senate Foreign Relations Committee, is to my mind much preferable.

## V

Our State Department has excused its failure to concern itself with social revolutions and political change by stating that we could not interfere in the internal affairs of other countries. Because in our own struggle for independence we desired to be let alone, it is natural that we should desire to refrain from interfering in the affairs of other nations, and that our representatives should write a strong statement to this effect in the articles of the Organization of American States. However, the minute we took over the responsibility of world leadership, this policy became unrealistic. We should have learned after a dozen years of foreign aid programs that we cannot give aid to another country without interfering in its internal affairs, since such aid is always interpreted by the political regime in power as an endorsement of it and used to strengthen and prolong its political power. Even to give technical assistance is in effect to foment an industrial revolution, which can be disruptive and bloody, as it has been at times in our own country. To trade with another country is to relate its economy to our policies on subsidies, import quotas, tariffs, stockpiling, surplus disposal, etc., to such an extent that in a smaller country any changes resulting from the whims of our legislators can have the direst internal consequences. We don't have a choice, therefore, between interference and noninterference, but only as to *how* we interfere. This is the responsibility of leadership.

But there is a better answer for the State Department. We have interfered consciously and intelligently in the internal affairs of certain other countries and the results have been beneficial to those countries and to us as well. One such case is the Philippines. Under the corrupt administration of President Elpidio Quirino, who became president in 1948, the Huks, members of an anti-Japanese guerrilla organization, were reactivated under Communist leadership to exploit the discontent of the farmers. The United States made known its dissatisfaction with the administration of Quirino and insisted on fiscal and other reforms as a requisite to further aid. Whatever were the good offices of the United States in persuading the two parties opposing Quirino in the 1953 election to join forces, they did so and elected Magsaysay as president. He quickly corrected the corruption and injustices and the Huk rebellion subsided, making it possible for the country to make rapid strides in development.

Greece, a strategic country in the Cold War, had been ravaged by the German occupation in World War II and in 1947 paralyzed by a Communist-inspired civil war, which was a reaction to the political turmoil that had sapped the vitality of Greece for forty years. During those four decades, the ruling king was once assassinated, twice abdicated, once deposed, twice died, and three times restored to the throne by plebiscite. There were three dictators, seven revolutions, and fifty governments. If we eliminate the only four-year period of regular government during that period, the ten years of Metaxas' dictatorship before the war, and the German occupation during the war, there were fifty governments in twenty-five years.

At the end of the first year's efforts of the American Mission for Aid to Greece to assist the Greeks in suppressing the guerrilla war and building up their economy, it was the testimony of those who were administering our aid program that the principal problems in Greece were political. The American ambassador, with State Department backing, refused to face the responsibility of giving political aid. Two years later, Greece was in such political turmoil that there were eight governments in one year and economic development was lagging. A new ambassador, John J. Peurifoy, whose prestige with Congress was such that he could be independent of the State Department, after a year's experience on the Greek scene, insisted that there must be political reform. Faced with this alternative or an end to American aid, the Greeks proposed a change in the election laws which would eliminate splinter parties and unstable coalition governments. This reform was endorsed publicly by Ambassador Peurifoy, but not without sharp criticism from the *Wall Street Journal* and the *Chicago Tribune* for "interfering" in the internal affairs of Greece. The election reform was approved, and since then Greece has had the longest period of stable government within the memory of its oldest citizen, and this, in turn, has made possible an amazing economic progress which is the envy of its neighbors behind the Iron Curtain.

An even more dramatic example of interference is the case of Puerto Rico. After Spain's colonial possessions in the Western Hemisphere were liberated at the end of the Spanish-American War in 1898, the United States decided that Cuba was large enough to handle its own affairs, and gave it independence and a guarantee of protection. Tiny Puerto Rico seemed too small to survive as an independent nation and so it was incorporated into the United States under the Organic Act of 1900 and given a status akin to a territory. Under this act and its revision in 1917, it was provided that in order to ensure good administration, the governor of Puerto Rico as well as three of the important cabinet ministers be appointed by the President of the United States. To ensure good legislation, it was provided that all statutes passed by the Puerto Rican legislature be subject to veto by our Congress. To ensure justice, our system of courts was established and Puerto Rico was placed under the jurisdiction of the judicial district of Boston. To ensure financial stability, we made our currency legal tender. To ensure literacy, we set up a system of public schools and provided teaching assistance. By removing any barriers to trade and travel, we brought about a cultural exchange which resulted in an understanding of our ideals and institutions. And perhaps most important of all, it became popular for Puerto Rican families who could afford to do so to educate their sons in American universities. In forty years time, social and political institutions were developed to the point that when a leader such as the present governor, Senor Munoz Marin, appeared on the scene with a program for raising the standard of living of the people, he was able to gain the intelligent support of the citizens and to find competent, educated leaders to carry out the program. The accomplishments have been spectacular.

Cuba on the other hand, basically a richer country, left to its own devices, was not able to rid itself of corrupt government, educate the mass of the people, or legislate social reforms. We interfered in Cuba by manifesting our friendship for Batista, who seized power illegally, suppressed all opposition ruthlessly, and enriched himself while disregarding the needs of the people. The Castro revolution rode into power with the support of the neglected "guajiros," and Castro turned to the Communists for help after it was denied by us. Cuba stands today in unhappy contrast to

Puerto Rico and as a monument to our failure to interfere constructively to help the majority of its people.

It is true that we have authority and power in Puerto Rico that we do not have in independent countries. To assist in bringing about changes in the latter will require greater ingenuity and finesse. It is also true that all three of the examples I have given are of countries that have shared our religious and cultural heritage. When we move into the continents of Asia and Africa, we will be among strange gods and customs, among ancient cultures and primitive cultures. As we try to help these people in their desire to short-cut the centuries of struggle which it took to lay our social and political foundation, we will have no blueprints and no experience to guide us. It is the greatest challenge any nation has faced. It is not the task for a few diplomatic dilettantes, flitting from country to country, but one which requires the concentration of dedicated men who are willing to devote a lifetime, if necessary, to helping a single country. It will require the enlistment of the best brains we have among our sociologists and political scientists and experts on related disciplines. Above all, it demands an understanding of the precepts upon which our country was founded and which have enabled it to become great, as well as a confidence that they are more vital and enduring than those of Communism. It will require a positive program of advancing these precepts, rather than a negative program of containing Communism, to win the Cold War. It will require a sense of mission and a willingness to sacrifice if we are to succeed.

# Hans J. Morgenthau

●

# PREFACE TO A POLITICAL THEORY OF FOREIGN AID

Of the seeming and real innovations which the modern age has introduced into the practice of foreign policy, none has proven more baffling to both understanding and action than foreign aid. The very assumption that foreign aid is an instrument of foreign policy is a subject of controversy. For, on the one hand, the opinion is widely held that foreign aid is an end in itself, carrying within itself a justification both transcending, and independent of, foreign policy. In this view, foreign aid is the fulfillment of an obligation which the few rich nations have toward the many poor ones. On the other hand, many see no justification for a policy of foreign aid at all. They look at foreign aid as a gigantic boondoggle, a wasteful and indefensible operation which serves neither the interests of the United States nor those of the recipient nations.

The public debate on foreign aid has contributed little to understanding. In the spring of every year, the nation engages in such a debate, carried on almost exclusively in terms of the amount of money to be spent for purposes of foreign aid rather than of the substantive purposes which a policy of foreign aid is supposed to serve. The Administration tries, as it were, to sell a certain amount of foreign aid to Congress, and Congress refuses to buy that amount. Congress generally appropriates about 10 per cent less than what the Administration has requested, and the Administration spends that amount as it sees fit within the general categories of the appropriation bill. It is only when glaring abuses and inefficiencies are uncovered, as for instance in our foreign aid to Laos, that the question of the substance of our foreign aid policy is raised in public, and even then it is raised in the negative terms of remedying the abuses and inefficiencies rather than in the positive terms of what the purposes of our foreign aid policy are supposed to be and what kinds of measures are best calculated to serve these purposes.

It is pointless even to raise the question as to whether or not the United States ought to have a policy of foreign aid. To ask that question is as pointless as to ask whether or not the United States ought to have a foreign political or military policy. For the United States has interests abroad which cannot be supported by military means and for the support of which the traditional methods of diplomacy are only in part appropriate. If foreign aid does not support them, they will not be supported at all.

The question, what kind of policy of foreign aid ought we to have, can then not be evaded. As it has developed in recent years, our policy of foreign aid is fundamentally weak. It has been conceived as a self-sufficient technical enterprise, covering a multitude of disparate objectives and activities, responding haphazardly to all kinds of demands, sound and unsound, unrelated or only by accident related to the political purposes of our foreign policy. The United States has been in the business of foreign aid for more than a decade, but it has yet to develop an intelligible theory of foreign aid that could provide standards of judgment for both the supporters and opponents of a particular measure.

### Six Types of Foreign Aid

The first prerequisite for the development of a viable philosophy of foreign aid is the recognition of the diversity of policies that go by that name. Six such policies can be distinguished which have only one thing in common: the transfer of money and economic services from one nation to another. They are humanitarian foreign aid, subsistence foreign aid, military foreign aid, bribery, prestige foreign aid, and foreign aid for economic development.

Of these different types of foreign aid, only humanitarian foreign aid is per se nonpolitical. The aid which governments have traditionally extended to each other in case of natural disasters, such as floods, famines, and epidemics, falls in that category. So do the services, especially in the fields of medicine and agriculture, which private organizations, such as churches and foundations, have traditionally provided in Asia, Africa, and Latin America.

While humanitarian aid is per se nonpolitical, it can indeed perform a political function when it operates within a political context. The foreign aid private organizations provide will be attributed for better or for worse to their respective governments insofar as humanitarian aid emanating from a foreign country is recognized by the recipient country to perform a political function. Thus the agricultural aid which the Rockefeller Foundation has provided for many years to certain Latin American countries is likely to take on under contemporary conditions a political function which it did not perform previously. The same has been true from the beginning of the work the Ford Foundation has been doing in India. By the same token, humanitarian aid extended by a government may have political effects.

Subsistence foreign aid is extended to governments, such as those of Jordan and Libya, which do not command the resources to maintain minimal public services. The giving nation makes up the deficit in the budget of the recipient nation. Subsistence foreign aid is akin to the humanitarian type in that it seeks to prevent the breakdown of order and the disintegration of organized society itself. It performs the political function of maintaining the status quo. It maintains it without, as a rule, increasing its viability. Where there is a political alternative to an unviable regime, subsistence foreign aid diminishes its chances of materializing.

Bribes proffered by one government to another for political advantage were until the beginning of the nineteenth century an integral part of the armory of diplomacy. No statesman hesitated to acknowledge the giving and accepting of bribes. Thus it was proper and common for a government to pay the foreign minister or ambassador of another country a pension, that is, a bribe. Lord Robert Cecil, the Minister of Elizabeth, received one from Spain. Sir Henry Wotton, British Ambassador to Venice in the seventeenth century, accepted one from Savoy while applying for one from Spain. The documents which the French revolutionary government published in 1793 show that France subsidized Austrian statesmen between 1757 and 1769 to the tune of 82,652,479 livres, with the Austrian Chancellor Kaunitz receiving 100,000.

Nor was it regarded any less proper or less usual for a government to compensate foreign statesmen for their cooperation in the conclusion of treaties. In 1716, the French Cardinal Dubois offered the British Minister Stanhope 600,000 livres for an alliance with France. He reported that Stanhope, while not accepting the proposition at that time, "listened graciously without being displeased." After the conclusion of the Treaty of Basel of 1795, by virtue of which Prussia withdrew from the war against France, the Prussian Minister Hardenberg received from the French government valuables worth 30,000 francs and complained of the insignificance of the gift. In 1801, the Margrave of Baden spent 500,000 francs in the form of "diplomatic presents," of which the French Foreign Minister Talleyrand received 150,000. It was originally intended to give him only 100,000, but the amount was increased after it had become known that he had received from Prussia a snuffbox worth 66,000 francs as well as 100,000 francs in cash. The Prussian Ambassador in Paris summed up well the main rule of this game when he reported to his government in 1802: "Experience has taught everybody who is here on diplomatic business that one ought never to give anything before the deal is definitely closed, but it has only proved that the allurement of gain will often work wonders."

Much of what goes by the name of foreign aid today is in the nature of such bribes. The transfer of money and services from one government to another performs here the function of a price paid by the former to the latter for political services rendered or to be rendered by the latter to the former. These bribes differ from the traditional ones, of which we have given examples above, in two respects: they are justified primarily in terms of foreign aid for economic development, and money and services are transferred through elaborate machinery fashioned for genuine economic aid. In consequence, these bribes are a less effective means for the purpose of purchasing political favors than were the traditional ones.

The compulsion of substituting for the traditional business-like transmission of bribes the pretense and elaborate machinery of foreign aid for economic development results from a climate of opinion which accepts as universally valid the proposition that the highly developed industrial nations have an obligation to transfer money and services to underdeveloped nations for the purpose of economic development. Thus, aside from humanitarian and military foreign aid, the only kind of transfer of money and services which seems to be legitimate is the one made for the purpose of economic development. Economic development has become an ideology by which the transfer of money and services from one government to another is rationalized and justified.

However, the present climate of opinion not only assumes that highly developed industrial nations have an obligation to extend foreign aid for economic development to underdeveloped nations. It also assumes as a universally valid proposition that economic development can actually be promoted through such transfer of money and services. Thus economic development as an ideology requires machinery that makes plausible the assumption of the efficacy of the transfer of money and services for the purpose of economic development. In contrast to most political ideologies, which operate only on the verbal level and whose effects remain within the realm of ideas, this political ideology, in order to be plausible, requires an elaborate apparatus serving as an instrument for a policy of make-believe. The government of nation A, trying to buy political advantage from the government of nation B for, say, the price of 20 million dollars, not only must pretend, but also must act out in elaborate fashion the pretense, that what it is actually doing is giving aid for economic development to the government of nation B.

This practice of giving bribes as though they were contributions to economic development creates of necessity expectations, in the giver and the recipient, which are bound to be disappointed. Old-fashioned bribery is a straightforward transaction; services are to be rendered at a price, and both sides know what to expect. Bribery disguised as foreign aid for economic development makes of giver and recipient actors in a play which in the end they can no longer distinguish from reality. In consequence, both expect results in terms of economic development which in the nature of things could not have been forthcoming. Thus both are bound to be disappointed, the giver blaming the recipient

74

for his inefficiency and the recipient accusing the giver of stinginess and asking for more. The ideology, taken for reality, gets in the way of the original purpose of the transaction, and neither side believes that it has received what it is entitled to.

Until recently, military aid took the lion's share of the foreign aid programs of the United States. A shift in favor of nonmilitary aid occurred during the 1961 session when Congress appropriated in excess of 2 billion dollars for military aid, while the total voted for all the other foreign aid programs amounted to in excess of 3 billion dollars. To the latter amount must be added approximately 1 billion dollars from the proceeds of the sale of agricultural commodities for foreign currencies to be used for economic grants and loans to purchasing governments.

Foreign aid for military purposes is a traditional way by which nations buttress their alliances. Rome used to receive tribute from its allies for the military protection it provided. The seventeenth and eighteenth centuries are the classic period of military subsidies by which especially Great Britain endeavored to increase the military strength of her continental allies. Glancing through the treaties of alliance of that period, one is struck by the meticulous precision with which obligations to furnish troops, equipment, logistic support, food, money, and the like were defined. The loans which France extended to Russia after the conclusion of the alliance between the two nations in 1894 fall in the same category. This traditional military aid can be understood as a division of labor between two allies who pool their resources, one supplying money, matériel, and training, the other providing primarily manpower.

In contrast to traditional practice, military aid is today not only extended to allies but also to certain uncommitted nations. The military aid the United States has been giving to Yugoslavia is a case in point. The purpose is here not so much military as political. It seeks political advantage in exchange for military aid. It obligates the recipient toward the giver. The latter expects the former to abstain from a political course which might put in jeopardy the continuation of military aid. Military aid is here really in the nature of a bribe.

What appears as military aid may also be actually in the nature of prestige aid, to be discussed below. The provision of

75

jet fighters and other modern weapons for certain underdeveloped nations can obviously perform no genuine military function. It increases the prestige of the recipient nation both at home and abroad. Being in the possession of some of the more spectacular instruments of modern warfare, a nation can at least enjoy the illusion of having become a modern military power.

As bribery appears today in the guise of aid for economic development, so does aid for economic development appear in the guise of military assistance. In the session of 1961, Congress, for instance, appropriated 425 million dollars for economic aid to strategic areas, and it is likely that in the total appropriations for military aid in excess of 2 billion dollars other items of economic aid are hidden. This mode of operation results from the reluctance of Congress to vote large amounts for economic aid in contrast to its readiness to vote virtually any amount requested for military purposes. Yet the purposes of aid for economic development are likely to suffer when they are disguised as military assistance, as we saw the purposes of bribery suffer when disguised as aid for economic development. The military context within which such aid is bound to operate, even though its direct administration be in the hands of the civilian authorities, is likely to deflect such aid from its genuine purposes. More particularly, it strengthens the ever present tendency to subordinate the requirements of aid for economic development to military considerations.

Prestige aid has in common with modern bribes that its true purpose, too, is concealed by the ostensible purpose of economic development. The unprofitable or idle steel mill, the highway without traffic and leading nowhere, the airline operating with foreign personnel and at a loss but under the flag of the recipient country—they ostensibly serve the purposes of economic development and under different circumstances could do so. Actually, however, they perform no positive economic function. They owe their existence to the penchant, prevalent in many underdeveloped nations, for what might be called "conspicuous industrialization," an industrialization spectacular in producing symbols of, and monuments to, industrial advancement rather than satisfying the objective economic needs of the country. This tendency sheds an illuminating light upon the nature of what is generally referred to as the "revolution of rising expectations."

We are inclined to assume that the "revolution of rising expectations," that is, the urgent desire to improve one's lot by means of modern technology and industry, is a well-nigh universal trend in Asia, Africa, and Latin America. Actually, however, this trend is universal only in the sense that virtually all underdeveloped nations want to appear as having achieved industrialization, while only a fraction of the population, and frequently only small elite groups within it, seek the social and economic benefits of industrialization and are willing to take the measures necessary to achieve them. For many of the underdeveloped nations the steel mill, the highway, the airline, the modern weapons, perform a function that is not primarily economic or military but psychological and political. They are sought as symbols and monuments of modernity and power. They perform a function similar to that which the cathedral performed for the medieval city and the feudal castle or the monarch's palace for the absolute state. Nehru is reported to have said, when he showed Chou-En-Lai a new dam: "It is in these temples that I worship." And the more underdeveloped and less viable a nation is, the greater is likely to be its urge to prove to itself and to the world through the results of prestige aid that it, too, has arrived in the mid-twentieth century.

The advantage for the giver of prestige aid is threefold. He may receive specific political advantages in return for the provision of aid, very much after the model of the advantage received in return for a bribe. The spectacular character of prestige aid establishes a patent relationship between the generosity of the giver and the increased prestige of the recipient. The giver's prestige is enhanced, as it were, by the increase of the recipient's prestige. Finally, prestige aid comes relatively cheap. A limited commitment of resources in the form of a spectacular but economically useless symbol of, or monument to, modernity may bring disproportionate political dividends.

The giver of foreign aid must perform the task of distinguishing between prestige aid and aid for economic development. It is in the nature of prestige aid that it is justified by the prospective recipient in terms of genuine economic development. The prospective giver, unaware of the distinction, is likely to fall into one of two errors. ~~By mistaking prestige aid for aid for economic~~ development, he will either waste human and material resources in support of the latter, while the purpose of prestige aid could have been achieved much more simply and cheaply. Or else he will reject out of hand a request for prestige aid because it cannot be justified in terms of economic development, and may thereby forgo political advantages which he could have gained from the provision of the prestige aid requested. The classic example of this error is the American rejection of the Afghan request for the paving of the streets of Kabul as economically unsound. It may be noted in passing that the Soviet Union, pursuing a politically oriented policy of foreign aid, paved the streets of Kabul, even though that measure had no bearing upon the economic development of Afghanistan.

## Foreign Aid for Economic Development in Particular

None of the types of foreign aid discussed thus far poses theoretical questions of the first magnitude; rather they raise issues for practical manipulation which can be successfully met by common sense tested by experience. Foreign aid for economic development has been the primary area for theoretical analysis and speculation, and these have been primarily of an economic nature. Economic thought, true to its prevailing academic tradition, tends to look at foreign aid as though it were a self-sufficient technical enterprise to be achieved with the instruments, and judged by the standards, of pure economics. And since Western economic development, from the first industrial revolution onwards, has been due to the formation of capital and the accumulation of technical knowledge, we have tended to assume that these two factors would by themselves provide the impetus for the economic development of the underdeveloped nations of Asia, Africa, and Latin America. This tendency has been powerfully supported by the spectacular success of the Marshall Plan, conceived and executed as a strictly economic measure for the provision of capital and technological know-how. Yet it is not always recognized that this success was made possible only by the fact that, in contrast to the underdeveloped nations of Asia, Africa, and Latin

America, the recipients of Marshall aid were among the leading industrial nations of the world, whose economic systems were but temporarily in disarray.

The popular mind, on the other hand, and, through it, much of the practice of foreign aid have proceeded from certain unexamined assumptions, no less doubtful for being deeply embedded in the American folklore of politics. Thus the popular mind has established correlations between the infusion of capital and technological know-how into a primitive society and economic development, between economic development and social stability, between social stability and democratic institutions, between democratic institutions and a peaceful foreign policy. However attractive and reassuring these correlations may sound to American ears, they are borne out neither by the experiences we have had with our policies of foreign aid nor by general historic experience.

The first of these assumptions implies that underdevelopment is at least primarily the result of lack of capital and technological know-how. Underdevelopment is regarded as a kind of accident or at worst as a kind of deficiency disease, which can be taken care of through the infusion of capital and technological know-how. Yet a nation may suffer from deficiencies, some natural and insuperable, others social and remediable, which no amount of capital and technological know-how supplied from the outside can cure. The poverty of natural resources may be such as to make economic development impossible. Nations such as Jordan, Libya, and Somalia are in all likelihood permanently incapable of economic development for that reason. Many of the nations which are the permanent recipients of subsistence aid are likely to fall in the same category.

A nation may also suffer from human deficiencies which preclude economic development. As there are individuals whose qualities of character and level of intelligence make it impossible for them to take advantage of economic opportunities, so are there nations similarly handicapped. To put it bluntly: as there are bums and beggars, so are there bum and beggar nations. They may be the recipients of charity, but short of a miraculous transformation of their collective intelligence and character,

79

what they receive from the outside is not likely to be used for economic development.

Some nations are deficient in the specific kind of character and intelligence which goes into the making of a modern economic system, but their general qualities of character and level of intelligence qualify them for the necessary transformation. They are, to use a rough analogy, in a medieval stage of cultural development, still awaiting the equivalent of the moral and intellectual revolutions which in the sixteenth and seventeenth centuries created the cultural preconditions for the economic development of the West. Yet we tend to take the existence of these preconditions for granted, forgetting that without the secularization and rationalization of Western thought and society the industrialization of the West would not have been possible.

A civilization, such as the Burmese, which deprecates success in this world because it stands in the way of success in the other world, puts a cultural obstacle in the path of industrial development, which foreign aid by itself cannot overcome. Saving, that is, the preservation of capital or goods for future use, has become so integral a part of our economic thought and action that it is hard for us to realize that there are hundreds of millions of people in the underdeveloped areas of the world who are oblivious of this mode of operation, indispensable to economic development. We have come to consider the productive enterprise as a continuum in which the individual owner or manager has a personal stake. Yet in many underdeveloped areas the productive enterprise is regarded primarily as an object for financial exploitation, to be discarded when it has performed its function of bringing the temporary owner a large financial return in the shortest possible time. Foreign aid poured into such a precapitalistic and even prerational mould is not likely to transform the mould, but rather it will be forced by the mould into channels serving the interests of a precapitalistic or prerational society.

The economic interests which stand in the way of foreign aid being used for economic development are typically tied in with the distribution of political power in underdeveloped societies. The ruling groups in these societies derive their political power in good measure from the economic *status quo*. The ownership and control of arable land, in particular, is in many of the underdeveloped societies the foundation of political power. Land reform and industrialization are in consequence an attack upon the political *status quo.* In the measure that they are successful, they are bound to affect drastically the distribution of economic and political power. Yet the beneficiaries of both the economic and political *status quo* are the typical recipients of foreign aid given for the purpose of changing the *status quo!* Their use of foreign aid for this purpose requires a readiness for self-sacrifice and a sense of social responsibility which few ruling groups have shown throughout history. Foreign aid proffered under such circumstances is likely to fail in its purpose of economic development and, as a bribe to the ruling group, to strengthen the economic and political *status quo.* It is likely to accentuate unsolved social and political problems rather than bring them closer to solution. A team of efficiency experts and public accountants might well have improved the operations of the Al Capone gang; yet by doing so, it would have aggravated the social and political evils which the operations of that gang brought forth.

Given this likely resistance of the ruling group to economic development, foreign aid requires drastic political change as a precondition for its success. Foreign aid must go hand in hand with political change, either voluntarily induced from within or brought about through pressure from without. The latter alternative faces the giving nation with a dual dilemma. On the one hand, to give foreign aid for economic development without stipulating conditions that maximize the chances for success maximizes the chances for failure. On the other hand, to give aid "with strings" arouses xenophobic suspicions and nationalistic resentments, to be exploited both by the defenders of the *status quo* and the promoters of Communist revolution.

Furthermore, once one has decided upon bringing about political change in opposition to the ruling group, one must identify the alternative group as the instrument of political change. Sometimes, one may have a choice among different alternative groups equally unattractive. Sometimes, and not infrequently, the absence of any alternative group either forces one to create one or else leaves one no choice.

Finally, the promotion of drastic social change on the part of the giving nation creates the precondition for economic development, but it also conjures up the spectre of uncontrollable revolution. In many of the underdeveloped nations, peace and order are maintained only through the ruthless use of the monopoly of violence by the ruling group. Determined and skillful foreign intervention may not find it hard to weaken the power of the ruling group or to remove it from power altogether. While it may be able to control events up to this point, that is, to instigate drastic reform and revolution, it may well be unable to control the course of the revolution itself. More particularly, a democratic nation, such as the United States, is greatly handicapped in competing with Communists in the control of the revolution. The revolution may start, as did the Cuban revolution, under the democratic auspices of the unorganized masses dedicated to social reform and supported by the United States, and may in the course of its development be taken over by the highly organized and disciplined Communist minority, the only organized and disciplined revolutionary group available.

Successful foreign aid for economic development may have similarly unsettling political results. Economic development, especially by way of industrialization, is likely to disrupt the social fabric of the underdeveloped nation. By creating an urban industrial proletariat, it loosens and destroys the social nexus of family, village, and tribe, in which the individual had found himself secure. And it will not be able, at least not right away, to provide a substitute for this lost social world. The vacuum thus created will be filled by social unrest and political agitation. Furthermore, it is not the downtrodden masses living in a static world of unrelieved misery which are the likely protagonists of revolution, but rather those groups that have begun to rise in the social and economic scale but not enough to satisfy their aroused expectations. Thus, economic development is bound to disturb not only the economic *status quo* but, through it, the political *status quo* as well. If the change is drastic enough, the social and political effects of economic development may well amount to a prerevolutionary or revolutionary situation. And while the United States may have started the revolutionary process, it will again be uncertain under whose auspices it will be ended.

The United States faces a number of formidable handicaps in the performance of the task of controlling social and political change in the underdeveloped nations either as a prerequisite for, or a result of, foreign aid for economic development. First of all, the United States is a Western capitalistic nation. It is a conservative power both domestically and internationally, and must so appear particularly to the underdeveloped nations. Both in its civilization and social and economic structure, it belongs to that complex of nations which until recently were able to hold Africa, Latin America, and the outlying areas of Asia in a condition of colonial or semicolonial dependency. It has military alliances with these nations, and while it has generally shunned and even opposed outright colonial policies, it has actively and successfully participated in the semicolonial exploitation of backward nations. Thus the resentment against the former colonial powers attaches also to it, and its policies of foreign aid are frequently suspected as serving in disguise the traditional ends of colonialism.

Furthermore, the United States, by dint of its pluralistic political philosophy and social system, cannot bring to the backward nations of the world a simple message of salvation, supported first by dedicated and disciplined revolutionary minorities and then by totalitarian control. In the nature of things the advantage lies here with the Communist powers. They are, as it were, specialists in exploiting a revolutionary situation, which is bound to cause us embarrassment. For while the Communists are able to direct a revolution into the desired channels through their use of a disciplined minority, we, even if we are convinced that revolution is inevitable and therefore do not oppose it, tend to look with misgivings upon it since we cannot control the direction it will take.

The Communist powers have still another advantage over the United States in that their problems and achievements are more meaningful, at least on the surface, to the underdeveloped nations than are ours. The Soviet Union has achieved, and Communist China attempts to achieve, what the more enlightened underdeveloped nations seek: a drastic increase in the standard of living through rapid industrialization. The Communist powers use totalitarian control as their instrument and Communist doctrine as rationalization and justification. Seeking the same results, the underdeveloped nations cannot help being attracted by the methods which brought these results about elsewhere. In contrast, the slow process, stretching over centuries, through which the nations of the West achieved a high standard of living through industrialization must appeal much less to them. That appeal is lessened even more by the economic processes of the free market and the political processes of liberal democracy through which in large measure Western industrialization was achieved. For these processes require a degree of moral restraint and economic and political sophistication which are largely absent in the under-developed nations. The simple and crude methods of totalitarian-ism must appear to them much more congenial.

Thus we arrive at the disconcerting conclusion that successful foreign aid for economic development can be counterproductive if the social and political goal of the giving nation is the recipient's social and political stability. In some cases at least, the failure of American aid for economic development may have been a blessing in disguise in that it did not disturb a stable *status quo* whose continuing stability was our main interest. Such aid, in-tended for economic development, actually performs the function either of a bribe or of prestige aid. Here again, however, these functions are likely to be impaired by disappointed expectations of economic development of the giving and the recipient nation.

It is equally a moot question whether or not successful foreign aid for economic development is conducive to the development of democratic institutions and practices. This is obviously not the place to raise *ex professo* the issue of the relationship between democracy and economic development. But that no necessary relationship exists between the two, recent history has made clear. The most impressive example is the Soviet Union. Its rapid eco-nomic development has gone hand in hand with totalitarian government, and a case could well be made for the proposition that the former would have been impossible without the latter. It is more likely than not that where the intellectual and moral preconditions for economic development are lacking in the pop-ulation at large and are present only in a small elite, as they are in many of the underdeveloped nations, the imposition of the will of that small minority upon the majority of the population is not only a precondition for the start of economic development but also for sustained economic growth.

## Preface to a Political Theory of Foreign Aid

As concerns the promotion of a peaceful foreign policy, economic development is likely to be counterproductive, provided a political incentive for a belligerent foreign policy is present. The contrary conclusion derives from the popular, yet totally unfounded assumption that "poor" nations make war on "rich" nations for economic advantage and that "rich" nations are by definition peaceful because they have what they want. In truth, of course, most wars have been fought not for economic but political advantage, and, particularly under modern technological conditions, only economically advanced nations are capable of waging modern war. We did not consider the Soviet Union a military threat as long as it was economically underdeveloped; it became such a threat at the very moment its economic development had transformed it into a modern industrial power. Similarly, Communist China today is only a potential military threat by virtue of its economic potential, both likely to be activated by economic development.

Foreign aid for economic development, then, has a very much smaller range of potentially successful operation than is generally believed, and its success depends in good measure not so much upon its soundness in strictly economic terms as upon intellectual, moral, and political preconditions, which are not susceptible to economic manipulation, if they are susceptible to manipulation from the outside at all. Furthermore, the political results of successful foreign aid for economic development may be either unpredictable or counterproductive in terms of the political goals of the giving nation. In any event, they are in large measure uncontrollable. Foreign aid proffered and accepted for purposes of economic development may turn out to be something different from what it was intended to be, if it is not oriented toward the political conditions within which it must operate. Most likely, it will turn out to be a bribe or prestige aid, or else a total waste. To do too much may here be as great a risk as to do too little, and "masterly inactivity" may sometimes be the better part of wisdom.

### Conclusions for Policy

The major conclusions for policy to be drawn from this analysis are three: the requirement of identifying each concrete situation in the light of the six different types of foreign aid and of choosing the quantity and quality of foreign aid appropriate to the situation; the requirement of attuning, within the same concrete situation, different types of foreign aid to each other in view of the over-all goals of foreign policy; and the requirement of dealing with foreign aid as an integral part of political policy.

The task of identifying concrete situations in view of the type of foreign aid appropriate to them is a task for country and area experts to perform. Can this country not survive without foreign aid? Is its government likely to exchange political advantages for economic favors? Would our military interests be served by the strengthening of this nation's military forces? Does this country provide the noneconomic preconditions for economic development to be supported by foreign aid? Are our political interests likely to be served by giving this nation foreign aid for purposes of prestige? Can a case be made for foreign aid in order to alleviate human suffering? What kind and quantity of foreign aid is necessary and sufficient to achieve the desired result?

To answer these questions correctly demands first of all a thorough and intimate knowledge and understanding of the total situation in a particular country. But it also requires political and economic judgment of a very high order, and it does so in two different areas. On the one hand, it is necessary to anticipate the susceptibility of the country to different kinds of foreign aid and their effects upon the country. On the other hand, when this task has been performed, it is then necessary to select from a great number of possible measures of foreign aid those which are most appropriate to the situation and, hence, most likely to succeed.

In most situations, however, the task is not that simple. Typically, an underdeveloped country will present a number of situations calling for different types of foreign aid to be given simultaneously. One type of foreign aid given without regard for the effects it may have upon another type risks getting in the way of the latter. One of the most conspicuous weaknesses of our past foreign aid policies has been the disregard of the effect different types of foreign aid have upon each other. Bribes given to the ruling group, for instance, are bound to strengthen the political and economic *status quo*. Military aid is bound to have an impact upon the distribution of political power within the receiving country; it can also have a deleterious effect upon the economic system, for instance, by increasing inflationary pressures. Similarly, the effect of subsistence foreign aid is bound to be the support of the *status quo* in all its aspects. Insofar as the giving nation desires these effects or can afford to be indifferent to them, they obviously do not matter in terms of its over-all objectives. But insofar as the giving nation has embarked upon a policy of foreign aid for economic development which requires changes in the political and economic *status quo*, the other foreign aid policies are counterproductive in terms of economic development; for they strengthen the very factors which stand in its way.

This problem is particularly acute in the relations between prestige aid and aid for economic development. The giving nation may seek quick political results and use prestige aid for that purpose; yet it may also have an interest in the economic development of the recipient country, the benefits of which are likely to appear only in the distant future. Prestige aid is at best only by accident relevant to economic development; it may be irrelevant to it, or it may actually impede it. What kind of foreign aid is the giving country to choose? If it chooses a combination of both it must take care to choose an innocuous kind of prestige aid and to promote economic development the benefits of which are not too long in coming. Afghanistan is the classic example of this dilemma. The Soviet Union, by paving the streets of Kabul, chose a kind of prestige aid that is irrelevant to economic development. The United States, by building a hydroelectric dam in a remote part of the country, chose economic development, the very existence of which is unknown to most Afghans and the benefits of which will not appear for years to come.

It follows, then, from the very political orientation of foreign aid that its effect upon the prestige of the giving nation must always be in the minds of the formulators and executors of foreign aid policies. Foreign aid for economic development, in particular, whose benefits to the recipient country are immediate and patent is a more potent political weapon than one whose benefits are obscure and lie far in the future. Furthermore, the political effects of foreign aid are lost if its foreign source is not obvious to the recipients. For it is not aid as such or its beneficial results that creates political loyalties on the part of the recipient, but the positive relationship that the mind of the recipient establishes between the aid and its beneficial results, on the one hand, and the political philosophy, the political system, and the political objectives of the giver, on the other. That is to say, if the recipient continues to disapprove of the political philosophy, system, and objectives of the giver, despite the aid he has received, the political effects of the aid are lost. The same is true if he remains unconvinced that the aid received is but a natural, if not inevitable, manifestation of the political philosophy, system, and objectives of the giver. Foreign aid remains politically ineffectual as long as the recipient says either: "Aid is good, but the politics of the giver are bad"; or "Aid is good, but the politics of the giver—good, bad, or indifferent—have nothing to do with it." In order to be able to establish a positive psychological relationship between giver and recipient, the procedures through which aid is given, and the subject matter to which it is applied, must lend themselves to the creation of a connection between aid and the politics of the giver which reflects credit upon the latter.

The problem of foreign aid is insoluble if it is considered as a self-sufficient technical enterprise of a primarily economic nature. It is soluble only if it is considered an integral part of the political policies of the giving country, which must be devised in view of the political conditions, and for its effects upon the political situation, in the receiving country. In this respect, a policy of foreign aid is no different from diplomatic or military policy or propaganda. They are all weapons in the political armory of the nation.

As military policy is too important a matter to be left to the generals, so is foreign aid too important a matter to be left to the economists. The expertise of the economist must analyze certain facts, devise certain means, and perform certain functions of manipulation for foreign aid. Yet the formulation and overall execution of foreign aid policy is a political function. It must be performed by the political expert.

It follows from the political nature of foreign aid that it is not a science but an art. What that art requires by way of mental predisposition is political sensitivity to the interrelationship among the facts, present and future, and ends and means. The requirements by way of mental activity are twofold. It requires first of all a discriminatory judgment of facts, ends, and means and their effects upon each other. However, an analysis of the situation in the recipient country and, more particularly, its projection into the future and the conclusions from the analysis in terms of policy can only in part be arrived at through rational deduction from ascertainable facts. When all the facts have been ascertained, duly analyzed, and conclusions drawn from them, the final judgments and decisions can be derived only from subtle and sophisticated hunches. The best the formulator and executor of a policy of foreign aid can do is to maximize the chances that his hunches turn out to be right. Here as elsewhere in the formulation and conduct of foreign policy, the intuition of the statesman rather than the knowledge of the expert will carry the day.

# Max F. Millikan

•

# THE POLITICAL CASE FOR
# ECONOMIC DEVELOPMENT AID

Our experience with foreign aid as an important instrument of United States policy toward the underdeveloped countries is limited to the few years since World War II. As with any new tool, we have been experimenting with it, and have discovered over the past decade a surprising number of uses to which it could be put. There is considerable distress in many quarters, including some expressed by authors of other essays in this volume, that we have not developed a more adequate doctrine to guide the employment of this instrument. Something that might loosely be described as doctrine emerges from the annual attempt of the Executive Branch to extract from Congress an allocation of funds for foreign aid, and there has been increasing sophistication in the broad justifications put forward each year. But anyone close to the actual process by which decisions about individual projects and programs have been made in the past would be hard put to it to argue that these decisions flow simply and logically from a well understood set of first principles.

That there is no accepted way of even classifying the manifold purposes of our aid programs is apparent from a comparison of the three efforts at such classification made in the essays in this volume by Messrs. Chenery, Banfield, and Morgenthau, all three of them experienced and highly qualified students of our foreign aid programs. Mr. Chenery, as is appropriate for an official of the United States Agency for International Development (AID), uses in effect the most recent official classification of categories under which blocks of aid money are requested from the Congress, a vast improvement introduced in 1961 over the legislative categories used in earlier years. Three of Mr. Morgenthau's categories, aid for economic development, aid for subsistence, and aid for military purposes, appear superficially to parallel Mr. Chenery's three categories; but the correspondence is more apparent than real, and he adds three more. Mr. Banfield, who states explicitly that he is classifying doctrines and not uses, groups all of Mr. Chenery's categories and all but one of Mr. Morgenthau's under the heading of national security, which he divides into two broad subgroupings, indirect influence and direct influence, and then adds three more, two of which parallel Mr. Morgenthau's sixth or humanitarian purpose. I am sure Mr. Chenery would be the first to admit that recent decisions concerning the allocation of funds in each of the broad groupings voted by Congress reflect a variety of considerations much more complex than can be adequately dealt with by any of these schemes.

While these inadequacies of doctrine are distressing to the logical mind, they seem to me less surprising than some people find them. There are a number of good reasons for this state of affairs.

First, foreign aid is not a goal of the United States nor even a separable element in our foreign policy, but rather a handy multipurpose instrument of that policy which we have been tempted to use in an increasingly wide variety of ways for an increasingly broad range of purposes. Attempts to specify a single doctrine of foreign aid are like attempts to construct a doctrine which will relate all the uses of a screwdriver to the ultimate objectives the user may have in mind before one has available a catalogue of all types of mechanical equipment and of all kinds of malfunctioning of each. I am not saying the attempt should not be made. One must decide how many screwdrivers of each type to order. But we should not be surprised if the early attempts are a bit primitive.

The second reason for confusion is that foreign aid is one of the instruments we use in our relations with the so-called underdeveloped countries. With the exception of a few policies, like the Monroe Doctrine and the Open Door in China, we have only very recently come to feel that we needed to have policies toward the underdeveloped countries and that these policies were an important part of the complex of American foreign policy. We have just begun to worry about the nature of the forces at work in those societies, about our interest in the direction those forces take, and about what instruments we can use to influence that direction. The scholarly community has paid the most attention to date to the first of these factors, the nature of the transitional process through which the underdeveloped countries are going. It has paid least attention to the third, the possible character, scope, and limitations of detailed United States influence.

This is related to the third source of confusion about systematic foreign aid doctrine, namely our hesitation and embarrassment in thinking seriously about American manipulation of foreign cultures. Our hesitation reflects a very proper concern for the sensitivities of other peoples, who do not like to be manipulated, and our embarrassment reflects our long immersion in the doctrine of nonintervention in the internal affairs of other states. The facts of American power and pervasive influence throughout the world make this hesitation and embarrassment irrational, as I shall try to explain in more detail presently, but they have nonetheless understandably inhibited serious academic attention to these problems.

There is a final reason why we have not developed a more satisfactory aid doctrine. In view of the variety and complexity of the situations in which the aid instrument has been used in the past and will inevitably be used in the future, I am convinced that doctrine which will provide useful guidance to the aid administrator can be developed much more satisfactorily by an inductive process of generalizing from detailed case studies of a large number of particular situations than from any broad a priori reasoning. I would defend the utility of some of the superficial philosophizing about aid objectives in which persons like myself have indulged in the past as an essential first step in the infinite series of successive approximations from the grossly oversimplified to the realistically complex by which the public in a democracy must be brought to an understanding of the foreign policies of its government.

I would also defend as a second step the kind of sharp challenge to the emerging clichés of this first phase of doctrine building which is represented by the essays of Mr. Morgenthau and especially Mr. Banfield in this volume. To have a set of plausible generalizations sharply challenged, even when as in this case the challenge consists of no more than the assertion of contrary propositions of at least as little a priori validity, may serve the purpose of nudging the dialogue to a higher level of sophistication. A first step in prompting a more detailed examination of the circumstances in which it is true that "external capital will often make the critical difference between an upward spiral of economic, social, and political development and a downward spiral of stagnation and decay"[1] may be to assert equally flatly that, "Where cultural conditions do not allow of it, economic development will not take place, no matter how much aid is given. On the other hand, where cultural conditions are right for it, development will occur rapidly in the absence of any aid."[2]

There are circumstances in which each of these propositions has some validity, and I would argue that the debate cannot be advanced very far unless these circumstances are extensively elaborated by a detailed study of particular cases. I would agree heartily with the proposition advanced by both skeptics in this symposium that the debate to date has notably failed to come to grips with the most critical doctrinal issues on which improvement of the aid process depends.

But this poses a dilemma for me in the present essay. There is no room here to move the dialogue a significant distance into the third phase of detailed inductive examination of American foreign policy toward particular countries which would constitute the only really effective answer to Mr. Banfield's usefully corrosive skepticism about the aid optimists. On the other hand the American public and the American Congress must continue to make decisions about aid appropriations pending the emergence of a more satisfactory aid doctrine. Should Mr. Banfield's strictures prevail, we would be deprived of much of the experimental evidence on which that better doctrine must be built. Accordingly I am moved to offer a few comments on the skeptical position in an effort to support my view that pending the assembly of much more evidence and the elaboration of case by case an-

---

[1] M. F. Millikan and W. W. Rostow, *A Proposal: Key to an Effective Foreign Policy* (New York: Harper and Brothers, 1957), p. 56.

[2] Edward C. Banfield, "American Foreign Aid Doctrines," p. 13.

alyses of a kind that neither side of the debate has yet produced, the continuation of a substantial aid program along somewhat the same lines as the present Kennedy Administration's effort is a good bet for the United States.

The part of the argument to which I would like particularly to address myself has to do with that element in aid doctrine to which the new administration has given greatly added emphasis, namely that part which in Mr. Chenery's words justifies aid "to produce the kind of political and economic environment in the world in which the United States can best pursue its own social goals." This is very close to what Mr. Morgenthau calls aid for economic development and what Mr. Banfield identifies as the doctrine of indirect influence. Far from arguing that this is the only valid justification for the use of the aid instrument, I regard it as but one of many uses whose relationships to each other need more careful study and some of which may in particular instances give rise to conflicts which may have to be resolved in the light of the circumstances of the individual case.

The argument over the doctrine of indirect influence revolves around whether the United States can through judicious use of the aid instrument significantly influence the process of modernization through which the underdeveloped countries are going in ways which will bring their evolution into greater consonance with United States interests over the next couple of decades than would otherwise be the case. Messrs. Banfield and Morgenthau both argue that an affirmative answer can be given only if it can be demonstrated that aid will produce significant economic development, that development will produce social stability and democracy, that these will insure peace, and that peace is what we want. Mr. Morgenthau argues that much of our foreign aid is wasted since it does not take the noneconomic conditions for economic development sufficiently into account. Mr. Banfield takes the more extreme position that since each of the links in this chain is either exceedingly weak or nonexistent, the converse of the proposition is valid; that is, that since aid for economic development has a very small probability of achieving the results we want it is probably not worth its economic and noneconomic cost.[3] He then goes on to examine the consequences of the alterna-

[3] Edward C. Banfield, *op. cit.*, pp. 11 ff.; Hans J. Morgenthau, "Preface to a Political Theory of Foreign Aid," pp. 79 ff.

tive of no aid, and argues that United States withdrawal might under some circumstances be less damaging to United States economic and military interests than attempts to intervene which, in his view, are very likely to be unsuccessful.

This way of formulating the case for United States assistance to the long-range economic development of the underdeveloped countries seems to me to miss some of the most essential features of that case. While I would argue that each of the links is in fact a good deal stronger than Mr. Banfield contends, I think the most fruitful procedure is to try to restate the positive case in slightly different terms, relating it to Mr. Banfield's argument as we go along. I would like to reverse his sequence, starting with the threat to the United States interest posed by the prospective course of evolution in the underdeveloped world and working backward to ways in which a skillful use of the aid instrument by the United States might, over a period of time, reduce that threat.

The option of withdrawal posed by Mr. Banfield does not seem to me at the present moment in history to be a real option. It has indeed, as he asserts, become a cliché that the radical changes in the communication of ideas, people, and goods throughout the world community brought about by the technological revolution of the last half century have so increased the interdependence of the various parts of the world that isolation is no longer a real alternative for the United States. The fact that it has become a cliché does not mean that it is wrong. It may rather be so self-evidently true that it is not very interesting to debate whether the powerful historical forces operating to connect the most distant parts of the world more closely with each other are at this stage reversible.

Since World War II, with the exception of Berlin and perhaps Quemoy and Matsu, all of the crises which have occupied the attention of American foreign policy-makers have had their origins in the underdeveloped world. Our concern with Korea, Vietnam, Suez, the Congo, Algeria, Cuba—merely to start the list—has not been the result of a perverse insistence of American policy-makers of all parties on dabbling in matters of no real interest to the United States but is rather an inevitable concomitant of our new and inescapable global political, military, economic, and cultural responsibilities. Whether we like it or not, and whatever policies our government pursues, this interdependence is going to increase, not decrease, over the next couple of decades. If, as I am inclined to do, we take increasing involvement of the United States all over the world not as a matter of policy choice but as historically inevitable, the dangers posed for us by gross instability and outbreaks of violence in the underdeveloped countries become very much more complex and pervasive than is suggested by Mr. Banfield's analysis.

Let us take our military position for example. He says that the worst that could happen to us would be Communist takeover of the underdeveloped countries and their organization into a bloc devoted systematically to our military and economic destruction. This seems to me only one of the more improbable threats that we confront. The most serious military threat to American security and welfare posed by the underdeveloped countries seems to me to be a rather different one. It is that out of the social and political conflicts within these areas consequent upon the modernization process crises will be generated which, because of American, European, and Soviet bloc involvements of many kinds, will escalate first into limited war and then potentially into nuclear exchanges. This is sometimes referred to as nuclear war by miscalculation, but this suggests too simple a pattern to be adequately descriptive of what I have in mind. As tensions and irritations mount and inflammatory incidents occur, the growing circle of parties to these disputes becomes increasingly committed by irreversible steps to an escalation of conflict to higher and higher levels. We can perhaps, as Mr. Banfield suggests, deter calculated nuclear attacks by determined enemies upon the United States by maintaining our own deterrent forces at adequate levels. In a world of nuclear proliferation, however, this kind of logical deterrent in a two-party game provides us very little protection against the step-by-step spread of local conflict into general conflagration.

This military danger is only one of the threats confronting us. Our future welfare will be increasingly dependent on international cooperation and on effectively operating international institutions in the economic, political, and cultural fields as well. This is not the place to spell out the nature of this dependence, but it too will be seriously threatened by widespread chaos and instability in any part of the world. This threat is more immediately menacing because some elements at least in the Communist world still see major opportunities for the advancement of their interests in the generation of instability in the underdeveloped countries and therefore use their influence to promote it wherever possible. But even if the East-West conflict were somehow to be resolved, the United States would have a powerful interest in promoting the emergence of stable, moderate states capable of meeting at least some of the new aspirations of their own populations and willing and able to play their role in an orderly and interdependent community.

While our interests are great, our capabilities of influence are severely limited. To understand them better we must take a look at the sources of the instabilities which we can confidently predict will trouble the underdeveloped world over the next two decades. They are associated with the process of modernization through which all these countries in varying degrees and at various stages have been going in recent years. This process did not begin abruptly. Its roots go back into the nineteenth century and earlier. But the tempo has accelerated by several orders of magnitude in the recent past.

Until this tempo of modernization quickened, the societies of the underdeveloped world were at their roots by and large quite stable. Sociologically, they exhibited, each in its own way, a fairly clear pattern of castes and classes broadly accepted by most groups in the population as natural and inevitable. There was very little mobility among these classes and a very low level of aspiration for such mobility. Anthropologically, group loyalties were concentrated on an extended family, a village, or a small tribe, which powerfully shaped the values and perspectives of its members. Politically, the conflicts for power at the national level, where nations existed, were limited to a very small elite and the bulk of the population was politically apathetic or inert. Economically, the rural areas in which the bulk of the population lived were minimally dependent on outside markets. These primarily subsistence economies were of course dependent on the vagaries of nature and the weather, but exhibited quite stable patterns of occupational structure and of agricultural technology. Psychologically, the small communities with which people associated themselves provided great security. People's perception of the alternatives open to them was exceedingly limited. The pressures for change were small for the bulk of the population because while living was hard it did not occur to most people that they had any options.

Modernization is changing all this. Its key characteristic is an enormous widening of perceived alternatives by a constantly growing fraction of the population. Sociologically, the less privileged classes no longer accept their status as part of the scheme of things. They now see as possible, if not for themselves at least for their children, movement outside the narrow bounds of their traditional place in the community. Anthropologically, the growth of cities, the spread of education, the expansion of trade, and the dramatic mushrooming of interregional communication have led to an abrupt challenge to old values, a weakening of the cement of traditional loyalties, and rising levels of restlessness and frustration. Politically, rapidly increasing numbers of people are seeking participation in the making of decisions they formerly left to a distant elite, so that even in totalitarian states the leadership is confronted with the necessity of building a much broader mass base for its power. National consciousness and a sense of national responsibility is still in most places grossly inadequate for the successful operation of a national polity. But the political apathy which characterized the bulk of the populations of the traditional society is rapidly disappearing.

Economically, patterns of production, of skill acquisition, of employment, and of exchange are in a state of flux. The self-sufficiency of local communities is breaking down and the cities are filling with people escaping from traditional agriculture but unable as yet to find jobs in the urban economy. Psychologically, the security of the traditional society is disappearing, the search for a new identity is intense, and new activities and new movements which promise to give significance to the lives of restless and footloose individuals have great appeal.

This brief rough sketch of some of the destabilizing forces at work throughout the underdeveloped world can do no more than suggest a few of the facets of a revolutionary process which has many varieties and many dimensions. We badly need many more detailed case studies of what is happening to the attitudes and aspirations of each of a wide variety of groups of people in each of a large number of emerging nations. The term "revolution of rising expectations" commonly applied to this phenomenon is often given a focus too narrowly economic. The rapidly changing frustrations, ambitions, and hopes spreading through previously largely inert segments of the societies of the underdeveloped world and giving rise to protest, revolt, and extremism cannot be quieted by an increasing availability of consumption goods. This is not the political purpose of economic development programs. What is required to reduce the explosiveness of the modernization process is a fundamental transformation of social structure, of loyalties and values, of modes of political participation, of opportunities for education, skill acquisition, and challenging employment, and of channels for constructive energies.

As I shall argue presently, well designed economic programs are, I believe, a necessary prerequisite for the development of the complex conditions in which viable modern societies can flourish. But the consumption effects are not the primary ones.

It may be helpful to look at the new problems posed for the political leadership of the underdeveloped countries by the forces at work in their societies. Their primary problem, whether they are demagogues concerned only with their own position and perquisites or statesmen devoted to the national interest, is to stay in power. This was a relatively simple problem in a traditional society with a well established hierarchical structure dominated by a small elite and supported by an apathetic and largely fatalistic mass. Power could be maintained by a skillful manipulation of personal loyalties and obligations supplemented where necessary by the use of a limited amount of force applied at the few places where it was needed. As the traditional society becomes disrupted by social, economic, and psychological change the problems of the leadership become very much more complex. As an increasing number of segments of the population are shaken loose from their traditional bonds and perceive new opportunities of influence and of the manipulation of their position, the sources of challenges to power multiply and become increasingly unpredictable. Protest begins to make itself felt among the rising middle classes, students, workers, the urban unemployed, and the peasantry. At the same time as the number of groups with some political awareness multiplies the interdependence of different sectors of the society greatly increases. This is partly the consequence of such economic factors as the extension of markets, the monetization of what was formerly subsistence production, and the increasing degrees of specialization in the functions performed by different groups in the society, partly a consequence of the greatly increased ease of communication among different segments of the society, and partly a result of the increasing interconnections between local and national political activity.

These two phenomena, the increasing number of sources of potential challenges to the power of the leadership and the increasing interdependence of all sectors of the society, pose new problems of the management of power for the leadership. They must find symbols which, for increasing numbers of people, will effectively override local and parochial interests and attach all groups more effectively to the national leadership. They must somehow see to it that in one way or another the society offers the newly emerging elements of the population an opportunity to participate in activities which have national purposes and thus connect these elements to the nation, which meet aspirations for new career patterns, and which provide chances for these new groups to use some of the new skills they are increasingly acquiring. In a broad sense the leadership must provide employment for its constituents, and that employment must have certain qualitative characteristics if there is not to be widespread frustration and instability.

The efforts of the leaders of the underdeveloped countries to meet these new and increasingly complex problems of unifying their societies under their leadership take a great many forms. In most of these efforts we can, oversimplifying greatly, perceive three elements. The first is an effort to maintain control over the ever widening circle of newly restless groups by perfecting the instruments of force and coercion and applying them ever more broadly and deeply throughout the society. The second is to try to focus the attention of the various segments of the population on real or fancied external threats to the dignity, integrity, and independence of the national state. The third is to try to build national consensus around constructive programs for the economic and social development of the country as a whole. All three of these elements are to be found in the strategies of virtually every leadership group in the underdeveloped world, but there are enormous differences in relative emphasis. Let us consider briefly some of the attractions and disadvantages of three alternative political strategies involving primary reliance on each of these three elements.

An emphasis on control by repression of dissent and by an extension of the instruments of force is likely to be characteristic of two quite different sorts of leadership. On the one hand traditional leaders, accustomed to employing the military or the police to keep individual challengers from the traditional elite circle in line, will find it perfectly natural to attempt to extend this method to new sectors of the population as they become politically active and indeed ultimately may be forced to try to extend it to the population as a whole. By opening military careers to wider and wider segments of the population, that is by democratizing the military, this technique may for a time provide some outlets for the energies of newly restless men and some upward mobility for those who have begun to chafe under the limitations imposed upon them by their traditional status. As a short-term measure in the fairly early stages of modernization this kind of forceable control by the traditional elite may be quite effective.

In the longer run, however, exclusive reliance upon it is likely to prove difficult or impossible. As the instabilities inherent in modernization spread through the society, the maintenance of control by this technique requires an increasingly complex and dispersed military and police organization of a kind traditional elites have very little experience with. Beyond this a modern military establishment is almost everywhere itself a powerful modernizing force. The traditional elite following this route runs the serious danger that its own military establishment may turn upon it as has occurred in Iraq, Egypt, and Korea.

Heavy reliance is likely to be placed on this instrument also by a very different type of leadership, namely by a revolutionary elite which has come to power through the skillful manipulation of a dedicated and disciplined subversive organization, which may or may not be Communist. This kind of an elite which knows intimately from experience the tactics of opposition and resistance and which is likely to have an organization in intimate contact with the grass roots of the society is much better equipped, as Castro and Sekou Touré have discovered, to exercise comprehensive control.

# Max F. Millikan

Neither of these types of elite, however, is likely to be able to maintain stability over time as modernization proceeds through police instruments alone. The pressures of changing social, political, and economic aspirations are likely to mount in time to a point where protest gets beyond control. One of the great appeals of Communism to revolutionary elites is of course that it offers an organizational model for how to establish the kind of discipline in depth in all dimensions of the society that is necessary to forestall violent challenges to the leadership. While the Communists appear to have managed to pull this off with some success in a number of places to date, it seems to me doubtful whether many underdeveloped countries have even a potential leadership which could hold the rising forces of instability in line even with Communist help.

The appeal for national support against an external enemy has very considerable short-term advantages for the leadership, especially where, as in the ex-colonial countries, such an external enemy has been visibly present in the lives of a large part of the population over a considerable past period. During the colonial period the goal of establishing independence from colonial domination is a simple and clear one having considerable appeal to almost all groups in the population. As modernization proceeds, satisfaction of the new aspirations to which it gives rise can easily be made to appear dependent on the throwing off of the colonial yoke. The organization over time of resistance against the colonial power requires the development of the kind of discipline, the sort of grass roots organization, and the kinds of hierarchical lines of authority which will be useful in maintaining the power structure once its heights have been seized.

The difficulties begin to arise after the colonial power has withdrawn, when it is difficult for the leadership to keep the external threat real and meaningful to all segments of the population. The history of underdeveloped countries without a colonial experience and of those whose colonial era is receding into the past is replete with instances of attempts by the leadership to find substitute symbols of external danger. Economic influence, great-power domination, Leninist imperialism, and neocolonial politics have all been seized upon as potentially effective symbols by underdeveloped country leaders. Residual specks of colonial control (such as were West Irian and Goa) can be made to have much more domestic utility by a skillful leadership than their real importance to the nation would warrant.

But this kind of appeal is bound to be, over time, a wasting asset for the political leadership of an independent country. Increasingly people want to get on with the things independence was thought to be the condition for. The rising tide of demands for new patterns of living which the pressures of modernization bring with them cannot, I would argue, be stemmed indefinitely by external adventure or by appeals to an external threat. Without at least some elements of a real internal development program it seems to me unlikely that the leadership of most underdeveloped countries can avoid serious and often violent challenges to their continued exercise of power.

This is not to say that the third strategy of primary reliance on programs of internal construction and development can guarantee a leadership against extremist challenges to its rule. Internal development is a complex and difficult process, and even with substantial outside help the leadership may be incapable of making it work. There is the further danger that great emphasis on the symbols of growth and reform may stir the aspirations of the modernizers much more rapidly than actual development programs provide opportunities for them to participate in its realization. Even moderately successful development requires both administrative skills and political skills of a significantly higher order than those needed for the other two strategies.

High administrative skills are required because the number of things to be managed simultaneously for development is very great and reaches into every nook and cranny of domestic economy. As interdependence grows, breakdowns in the administration of any one of a large number of programs can menace the entire effort. Unusual political skills are required because to achieve its political purpose a development program must be designed to provide a wide range of kinds of opportunities for new activity to each major group in the society as its aspirations alter. If major groups fail to share not so much in the inevitably slowly expanding stream of goods and services as in the energy-absorbing and skill-utilizing activities which such a program generates, there will be the familiar cycle of rising frustration associated at first with apathy and then with an increasing resort to extremist views.

On the other hand, if development programs are even moderately skillfully handled by the leadership, they can have great political pay-off even in the relatively short run. India has demonstrated the symbolic appeal to an electorate of five-year development plans which have been brought close to the heart of politics in that country. A sense that the country is even very slowly beginning to move forward, that education is becoming more broadly available, that opportunities are opening up for small entrepreneurs, that school-leavers are able to find interesting employment, that rural communities can begin constructing new patterns of living—all these can have a significant impact on attitudes and hence on politics some time before substantial economic fruits of these activities begin to appear. Nonetheless, modernization is undoubtedly costly, and without at least slowly rising levels of gross national product the transformation of traditional societies, which is necessary to make them viable in the modern world, can probably not be brought about.

What I have attempted to argue up to this point is, first, that it is very much in the United States interest to do what we can to reduce the risks of chaos, instability, and violence in the underdeveloped world; and, second, that these risks are likely to be significantly less if the leaders of the underdeveloped countries devote a large share of their attention and their energies to promoting the internal economic, social, and political development of their national states.

I have said very little about democracy up to this point. Where does this link in Mr. Banfield's chain fit into my argument? I have argued not that development produces democracy and democracy produces stability, but rather that certain kinds of effective measures to promote development are in the long run a necessary prerequisite for reasonable stability. This is true whether the regimes in question are seriously attempting to build a society based broadly on consent or whether they are placing heavy reliance on totalitarian instruments of repression to contain disaffection. Thus I would argue that while in the absence of development democracy does not have much chance in the long run, the same may be said of authoritarianism. While this seems to me valid as a matter of objective prediction, it seems to me also highly likely that a leadership which has either not tried seriously to launch development activities or has tried and failed badly is going to be under very much heavier pressure both to adopt internally repressive measures and to experiment with external adventure, simply to maintain itself in power in the face of the rising frustrations among its constituents, than one which has launched even moderately successful development programs. While the prospects of these more disruptive strategies are also not good, in the absence of effective development the leadership has no alternatives.

I do not think I need to argue the case for the proposition that a commitment to forms of government that will take some account of the wants and interests of the major elements of the population is in the United States interest. The real question raised by Mr. Banfield is whether the prospects for finding leadership elements with this kind of commitment in a significant number of underdeveloped countries are sufficiently good to justify our devoting resources to supporting the economic development ambitions of potential leaders of this kind. Here I think Mr. Banfield grossly underestimates the strength and appeal of the democratic ideal among the rising generation in the non-Western world. We will certainly not see smoothly operating, fully democratic societies in any significant number of underdeveloped countries for at least several decades to come. The question is whether we can have a significant marginal influence on the rate of progress toward decentralized decision-making and toward governments in one way or another more responsive to the popular will. Here I think there is reason for considerable hope.

The thing that is surprising to me, observing the history of the last decade in Asia, Africa, and Latin America, is not how weak the forces for democracy have been but rather, in the light of all the difficulties Mr. Banfield points out, how strongly these forces have operated. While there is certainly no automatic connection between development and a trend toward democracy, and while I would oppose assisting the development efforts of regimes like the Communist Chinese which appear firmly committed to authoritarian techniques, the issue seems to me far from settled throughout most of the underdeveloped world, and the case is very strong for our helping to establish the economic and social conditions in which alone the spread of government by consent has a chance.

If a serious concentration of the efforts and energies of the leadership of the underdeveloped countries of the free world on economic and social development is indeed an important interest of the United States, it remains to be argued whether a vigorous American aid program can promote such a concentration and marginally increase its prospects of success. This is the first link in Mr. Banfield's chain. He gives a good part of his case away when he admits (page 13) that "there is an important middle group of countries . . . which can absorb large amounts of aid and which also show fair promise of eventual development." India, which he cites as an example, represents nearly a third of the total population of the underdeveloped countries of the free world. Something like a third of Indian capital formation is in turn currently made possible by the inflow of aid to India, a considerable part of which comes from the United States. Most foreign observers who have studied the Indian scene would agree that if this aid were cut off, the result would be not just a proportionate cut in the Indian growth rate but the stalling of the Indian development program, the depression of the private as well as the public sector of the Indian economy, a sharp drop in employment opportunities, and probably a severe decay of the internal political situation. While India is one of the most promising, one could select others with better than even present development prospects which would bring the population of this important group with high absorptive capacity for aid to over half of the population of the underdeveloped free world.

With respect to the remainder there are a few countries where most of what Mr. Banfield says is valid. Those parts of our foreign aid program which are devoted to economic development assistance should probably be more selective than they have been and should make a few dramatic demonstrations of our determination to withdraw economic development assistance where the local leadership is either unable or unwilling to try seriously to establish the conditions which will make the aid productive. But these two sets of countries—those like India where the leadership needs no incentive to press development programs but only the marginal resources to make such programs possible, and those which are clearly unable and unwilling to use aid effectively for development—do not exhaust the list. There is a large group of countries where the actual potential leadership is divided as to appropriate national strategy, some paying at most lip service to development goals and relying more heavily on instruments of force or symbols of external threat to maintain their power, and others genuinely and realistically eager to confront the hard task of internal construction. In these cases where the present development prospects may not be great, United States support and encouragement for the development-minded elements in the leadership may have considerable influence in focussing national energies on development efforts.

The interactions between economic, social, psychological, and political change are multiple and interdependent. Economic development partly requires and partly produces in a variety of ways the noneconomic circumstances which make further economic development possible. Mr. Banfield is of course right that there is no possibility of launching from the outside a modernization process for which there is no support from the internal forces at work in the society. But this is the situation in few if any of the underdeveloped countries. Most of them present a complex picture of some forces promoting and other forces resisting movement in a developmental direction. The secret of effective development assistance policy is to employ a kind of economic and political jujitsu, exploiting and reinforcing the constructive forces of modernization already at work on the local scene. This requires a much more sophisticated appraisal of the character of those forces than we now have available for many countries and a more skillful tailoring of our own instrument to them than we have achieved in the past. A careful appraisal of our potential influence can be made only on a detailed country-by-country basis. But to argue as Mr. Banfield does that it is a priori close to zero is as implausible as to argue, as some of the less cautious supporters of aid have done, that it can be decisive everywhere.

That modernization is on balance destabilizing, and economic growth difficult and at best uncertain, is certainly, as Messrs. Banfield and Morgenthau assert, incontrovertible. But these are risks inherent in the world environment in which we find ourselves which we can wholly avoid neither by offering aid nor by refusing to do so. The real question with respect to development aid is whether by skillful use of this instrument over a rather long period, say a decade, we can marginally influence the course of economic, social, and political modernization so as to reduce somewhat the risks with which it confronts us. In my view, the past decade of aid efforts, confused as it has been both in purpose and in execution, has produced political results which have been well worth the cost. With the new clarifications of doctrine currently being formulated in detail, our prospects for favorable influence seem to me much brighter. We shall certainly not avoid failures, crises, instability, and chaos in some parts of the world. But we have a fair chance of some notable successes which can make the whole effort enormously rewarding.

# Joseph Cropsey

●

# THE RIGHT OF FOREIGN AID

This essay addresses a question which can be stated with complete simplicity, but which, contrary to opinion, cannot be answered except with some difficulty. The question is whether a wealthy nation, say the United States, has a moral duty to extend aid to the undeveloped countries. Throughout, the attempt will be made to observe the distinction between duty and interest as strictly as possible. Whether it is to our interest to strengthen the economy or the military establishment of an undeveloped country is in large measure an empirical question, to be resolved by noting whether the recipient nations are in fact strengthened by our help, whether they become well affected toward us as a result of being helped by us, and so on. Whether, on the other hand, we have a duty to extend such aid is not an empirical question; one cannot point to facts and let them speak for themselves, prescribing our obligations to us. We can progress toward the answer only by reflection.

The question whether we have a duty to extend foreign aid is of special concern precisely because mere duty and interest, as different as another's benefit is from one's own, can easily conflict. We can never rest easy, nor be united in our policies, if the suspicion exists that what we do for others we do out of duty but against our interest. Moreover, not all men will be satisfied with policies that aim at our advantage but which appear at the same time to violate a duty to benefit other human beings. Because of the possibility that duty and interest will conflict, the grounds of each must be investigated in the light of the distinction.

In this paper, it will be assumed that if foreign aid should be contrary to our interest, there is a very strong presumption against giving it; and if it turns out to be to our advantage, there

is an equally strong presumption in favor of giving it. We shall
not take up the question as to whether it is in fact beneficial or
contrary to our interest. In either case it is necessary for us to
know whether there is a duty to extend it—a duty which is perhaps so compelling that we could be justly convicted of selfish-
ness and hypocrisy if we withheld it, notwithstanding the very
strong presumption against giving it if it is contrary to our interest.

The discussion that follows consists of four parts. The first
three parts take up, in turn, the three principles which are commonly appealed to, tacitly or openly, by those who speak of our
duty, or our moral duty, to give freely to the undeveloped populations. The first of these principles or grounds for giving is the
sentiment of fellow-feeling with others in their sufferings. It is
a fact that men are compassionate of the sufferings of other sentient
beings, and that they feel an impulse to be charitable. Our first
task is to take up the question whether the inclination to compassion or charity is rooted in our human nature in such a way
as to oblige us with the force of duty.

In the second place, we must consider whether the meaning
of the modern scientific project—the conquest of nature—does
not imply an obligation on the part of the advanced nations to
mitigate the miseries of the backward.

Thirdly, we must inquire whether our democratic principles
impose upon us, by virtue of their appeal to the rights of man, a
duty to all humanity whose cause is proclaimed in the Declaration
of Independence.

In the fourth part a resolution of the question is presented
in the form of a statement of the ground of our national duty,
somewhat different from those enumerated.

The question of policy before us is in some measure a theoretical one, and though this may be deplored it cannot be helped.
The practical issues are in fact questions of what it is right and
prudent to do in crucial conjunctures. Right and prudent always
have opposites. It is the task of high authority to discriminate
between the one course to be followed and the many courses to
be avoided, by ascending as far as need be to the truths that il-
luminate experience and transform it into understanding. It is
self-evident that age brings experience without fail, but understanding only in some cases. If facts do not speak for themselves,

we must put a pressure upon them. They stand in relation to us as patients, passive things or things acted upon; and we are the agents, the acting beings who operate with them. There is no other way to understanding. This truth does not stand in need of apology; but we must allow ourselves to be reminded that theoretical inquiry, like a proud servant, will not do its office where it is not made welcome.

### I

Wretchedness and poverty so far preponderate over well-being in the world that it is surely more feasible to count the comfortable than to measure the world's destitution. It is very fitting that the prosperous should give a thought to the miserable, and reflect on how the matter stands between them—what are the duties of affluence and what are the rightful claims of privation. As citizens in a wealthy nation, we learn something from the contempt in which men of means are held who take no pity on the worthy poor that come in their way. Further, among the wealthy we make a distinction. We do not admire, but we can concede something to the reasoning of the niggard who starts from his own frugality and concludes with a certain indifference to the privations of others. But how can we exculpate those who surfeit themselves, while under their feet the children of poverty learn the way of brutes in the school of starvation? We gratuitously insult the suffering as well as the opinion of mankind if we gormandize while a parent anywhere must stop his ears against the cries of his unfed young. Hunger accuses satiety, and comfort seems to owe an expiation to wretchedness.

The natural compassion of man reaches down to the faceless insects themselves. Darwin wrote of the pity he felt for a wasp struggling for life in the strands of a spider's net. The sympathy that we feel for the members of our race is only part of a sentiment we are capable of feeling for any sentient thing. Apparently there is a law of our nature that bids us relieve the sufferings of all things able to suffer, and certainly of our fellow-men wherever they may be. We appear to incline toward a universal charity.

If that inclination were sufficiently powerful in us, it would have as much the force of duty as our inclination and duty to multiply. The inclination toward a universal charity would confirm us in what we believe, apart from inclination or sentiment, to be our duty: we owe something to the other members of our species because of the similarity they bear to us. Like naturally goes together with like. Our care for others is part of our care for ourselves.

The scope of man's duty to man would appear thus to extend to the horizon. It is all-inclusive, comprehending everything that, like ourselves, can suffer. As soon as we say so, we are troubled by the failure of that rule to accord with many of the common practices of mankind which could not to a healthy mind appear objectionable. No one, for example, objects to the extinction of malaria-bearing mosquitoes or plague-ridden rats, although it is true that many men would be squeamish about themselves destroying the vermin which they know must be eliminated, just as they might be converted to vegetarianism if they had to slaughter the animals on whose flesh they gladly nourish themselves. It is clear that the sentiment of compassion a man can feel for the brutes' sufferings cannot be directly translated into a duty to the brutes on the mere ground of their being sentient things as we are. Our feeling about their feeling is in need of a rational correction, as we demonstrate by our use of them.

It is true that the brutes resemble us in being sentient; yet by our acts we evince our understanding that sentience does not put them upon such a level with us that we may not do with them as we see fit, even to taking away their lives for our bare convenience or pleasure. It is not their sentience or capacity to suffer pain and to fear death that determines our use of the brutes, but something else, perhaps reason, which is the basis of so profound a distinction between them and us that an assertion of their rights against us is unthinkable. If duties are the correlate of rights, then it is clear that as the brutes have no rights against their superiors in the order of nature, so men have no duties to them, notwithstanding their capacity for terror and pain. In the same sense in which a superhuman being could not be said to have a duty to man, man cannot be said to have a duty to the subhuman beings.

Certainly a man is to be blamed who cruelly abuses his brutes. Brutality is the name given to his offense; and by committing it he will arouse the indignation of a humane society. As the words brutal and humane imply, those who stand higher in the order of nature forfeit their station when they deal with the lower simply according to the way of the lower. It is amazing but true that if we did not begin by recognizing the inferiority of the brutes, we would not have the contempt for brutal men which becomes the ground for humane treatment of the brutes. It is important that this be understood, for it is a refutation of the belief that considerate behavior flows only from a duty in the agent which is correlative with rights in the patient; and that, rights existing only among equals, wherever there is to be considerate behavior, it is necessary to postulate the fundamental equality of the actor and the one acted upon—say, in that both have a strong love of life, or are equally capable of similar sentiments.

Our sympathy evidently reaches to myriad places in animate nature where we have no duties founded upon the rights of the sentient things that are acted upon. Moreover, bare sympathy or fellow-feeling is an imperfect guide to obligation for other reasons than those which are revealed by reflecting upon the status of dumb animals. For example, men compelled to observe the execution of a condemned criminal would certainly do so with some feeling; yet apart from any question as to the rightness of the verdict or the justice of the sentence, they would not feel a sense of duty to help him avoid his fate. The agitation engendered in a witness by the paroxysms of a strangling convict may be tantamount to an impulse to save him; but sympathy with the condemned man is overweighed by sympathy for his victim and other considerations, and the criminal is left to perish. Reason must arbitrate among the sentiments, or else actions become arbitrary—based ultimately on the pleasure and brute strength of the most violent men.

The suffering criminal exemplifies the human being whose pains are brought upon him by his guilt. But the suffering of the destitute may be brought upon them by misfortune rather than by anything for which they or anyone else could be responsible. What if not chance causes a blameless child to grow into a blameless but bad man in the midst of a natural waste? The land is poor and hunger is his portion, but through no one's fault: no one is responsible, not he nor any other human being. In truth, no one is responsible for the sufferings of men whose pains have their source in simple misfortune or chance. We would have a duty to the purely unfortunate at the other end of the world if duty were wholly unconnected with responsibility. To be responsible means literally to be answerable. He who is answerable for the ill is answerable for the remedy; but he who has only looked on intervenes to relieve the sufferer gratuitously, not out of duty. The intervention of the benefactor might make us love him; his indifference might make us loathe him; but his intervention cannot be demanded of him as a moral duty that is correlative with a right belonging to the one in misery.

This conclusion seems offensive to what ordinary humanity requires us to answer when we ask, Am I my brother's keeper? It is, however, not so obviously offensive to it as at first appears: for men conceive a care and affection for their brothers which they do not and cannot feel for unknown beings on remote continents. A man at the other end of the world cannot and ought not presume to claim what a parent, a brother, or a child might reasonably expect. That a man should keep his brother from harm is not to say that he is guilty as long as a human being anywhere exists who is poorer than himself. On the contrary, to acknowledge a duty of universal charity would be to enslave the rational and industrious to the rest. Worse than that, it would make an odious concession to the mere desire of the poor for comfort and wealth. The mere desire for prosperity, so far from deserving to be encouraged with alms, is in itself scarcely respectable, but is rendered more so by the industry and discipline that it brings on in those who labor to satisfy it. The desire for wealth which is not accompanied by the impulse to generate it through labor and forethought may be dismissed as a form of vulgar envy, made uglier by laziness. We conclude that a duty to relieve the suffering of our fellow human beings, for example through foreign aid, may not be deduced from the injunction of a sentiment of universal charity.

## II

We could thus leave the backward nations to extricate themselves from their difficulties as well as they can except so far as it benefits us to help them, if the duty of universal brotherhood meant simply the duty of universal almsgiving. But we are told occasionally that it means something far more than charity so narrowly understood. When we consider how man stands in relation to the whole of external nature, we appreciate how tight is the bond that draws into unison the members of our rational species. All together, we face external nature as a dual adversary: it is the enigma in which are wrapped the mysteries of our origins and our ends; and it is the inhospitable quarry from which we must gain the materials of survival and the equipment for a civilized life. Nature is both a riddle to the mind and a reluctant harvest in a stony field. We draw our theories and our subsistence from her grasp with almost equal difficulty. It has been said that the highest task of man, of mankind as a whole, is to establish its intellectual and technical supremacy in the world by conquering nature—discovering her secrets and turning her matter to human use. It is not a part but all of humanity that is bewildered and confined in the matrix of nature; it is the task, indeed the humanizing mission of man to emancipate himself from nature entirely. Only when he has penetrated to every significant truth—about matter, life, and disease, for example—and learned how to do whatever seems good to him—even to sowing human life on other globes in the outer spaces, and to remaking human nature itself—only then will man dominate his cosmic antagonist and dissolve the natural matrix that contains him. The freedom of mankind as a whole is imperfect as long as we are compelled to admit that there are things unknown to us and other things impossible.

The unity of mankind evidently need not be made to rest upon a vague and self-contradicting sentimentality, but rather can be inferred, it seems, from our status as a species in the order of nature. The function of man is to make use of his innate powers in order to realize his perfect freedom from bondage to nature. Perfect mastery of nature as the highest human possibility is the life-activity of the human species: it is our business on earth or beyond earth. In this task we participate as a species, for only a rational animal could conceive or execute such a plan, and all men participate in the rational nature of their species. On this ground the whole of mankind can be said to be one, and united in the contest with nature.

When science will have won its final victory, the argument for the universal responsibility of all men for all men will no longer be vulnerable to the rejoinder that only he who is answerable for the ill is answerable for the remedy. The blameless child who grows into the bad but blameless man in a barren waste will be relieved by science, which will abolish barren wastes, turning every desert into a garden, overcoming the mischances of individuals: chance will claim no more victims. The common human enterprise will bear fruit in a universal abundance which will bring relief to every human being, and every human being will be entitled to demand relief as his right because the mastery of nature is the work of humanity at large.

Swept on by the catholic benevolence of science, we are in danger of forgetting why we are engaged in discussing science. The reason is that the human kind is divided between the advanced and the backward. The backward are so, with respect to the standard of living surely, to say nothing of political influence, because science is an exotic among them. It belongs to and has its home among only some of the nations. No one knows where it may one day become domesticated; everyone knows that it now flourishes in the minor fraction of the human race. Science might be the human project in the sense described above only if it were the universal human project equally distributed among the peoples of the world.

Evidently a grave objection exists against beginning with the scientific project and ending, as if by inference from it, with universal benevolence in the form of a duty to extend foreign aid. The excellence of science and its essential human-ness are, as was said, intimately connected. If the emphatically human activity is science, then men stand higher in the order of humanity if they are more scientific, lower if they are less so. Alternatively, a more scientific nation is more civilized than a less scientific one. Science is not in fact the project of the whole human kind but of some parts of it more than others. The existence and the power of science do not point to a duty of the advanced and scientific peoples to relieve the backward; the existence and power of science simply raise again in another connection the question whether there is a duty of the more advanced to the less, based upon a genuine right of the less advanced. The elevation of science to the hope and the principle of humanity causes such a qualitative gap to open between the scientific and the subscientific parts of mankind that the subscientific portion's claim to consideration as a right is proportionally weakened.

## The Right of Foreign Aid

The scientific project is not, as such, the basis for a duty of the developed to the undeveloped. Nothing intrinsic to science requires the scientist to benefit the non-scientist rather than simply to benefit himself and his society—for his society is host to his laboratory—and to relieve his own estate to the utmost. If it be argued that the underprivileged will look on in a mood of deepening envy and resentment until they are ready to erupt in plunder, then the answer is, either repel them by the power of science under arms, or mollify them with whatever is needed to distract their restlessness. Such policies are intelligible and could easily be defended; but like the argument to which they are a reply, they have to do not with duty but with interest.

As it happens, there is a deeper reason for doubting that the scientific project points toward universal benevolence. That reason is the essentially qualified goodness of the scientific project itself, that is, of the absolute subversion of nature by man in the name of an unimaginable, transdemocratic because transpolitical freedom. Let us reconsider the meaning of the scientific conquest of nature, thinking first of the relation in which man and nature stand to one another. By nature we shall mean "the way all things are which men have not made," whether we can explain how or why they came to be so or not. Included in nature is also "the way men are," for certainly we are not our own creatures. Then nature, including human nature, is something that stands over against us, that has a way of its own, different from how we would have it if we had the making of it according to our own plan. The things we make we control, fashioning them to achieve some purpose or good of ours; but the unyielding things that exist according to a scheme not our own compel us to accommodate ourselves to them. We must plan our acts so that we do not dash ourselves against the intransigence of an uncompromising world.

As long, therefore, as man must take account of an unyielding "other," something which exists by a plan that is not his own and which refuses to lend itself to the purposes of his good pleasure; and which in fact will wound him or destroy him if he flaunts its tendencies—as long as man is opposed by such an "other," there is at least one firm criterion for judging the goodness of his own doings: he does well when, at the very least, he does not violate the conditions of existence laid down by that "other" with which he must coexist. And when that "other" is no less than nature itself, meaning the way man himself is and the way the universe external to man is, then the criterion of his well-doing is very comprehensive indeed. He is, so to speak, formed by the opposition of an unyielding "other" in the way that iron is formed against the anvil. The intractable "other" provides a frame of reference for judging of human actions by constituting the conditions within which all human action must occur.

As men we have the visible shape that we do because the inflexibility of the skeleton imparts it to us. In other ways our life is as it is because, for example, we cannot control the weather, the climate, and the sex of babies, to say nothing of the manner of our coming into being and the inevitability of our passing away. We are in thrall to nature, and our servitude is at the same time the fundamental condition of our lives and the background for judging whether we act ill or well. But the project of science is to throw off the bondage of nature, and to emancipate man by giving him autonomy in nature, with the understanding that autonomy in nature must mean rule over nature and nothing less. Perfect autonomy would mean the state of being absolutely unconditioned.

It is beside the point to rejoin that science seeks to discover the laws of nature and therefore aims at a more perfect obedience rather than at sovereignty. The nearest analogy to the case would be the discovery by a subject of the whole fundamental law of his king's behavior. Who can doubt that that subject would then be able to rule the king? He who masters the law of the lawgiver can master the lawgiver and take his place. There is no higher rule than that which governs the legislator.

When this is understood, we may perceive why in principle science cannot dictate a moral duty to relieve the backward. The meaning of science is given by its intention, not by the feasibility of that intention; and the intention of science is to liberate man utterly from the alien framework that controls, informs, and guides him. But an absolutely uncontrolled, uninformed, unguided being has no relation of obligation to any "other." And now it is of supreme importance to recollect that science is not the possession of all men but only of the scientists. Not mankind but those in possession of science would become the absolutely unconditioned beings. The profundity of the chasm between the scientific and subscientific people becomes obvious when we remember that the scientific conquest of nature includes the conquest, that is the reformation, of human nature. Those men who know how to remake man would have the power to transform the subscientific human beings into docile slaves as well as into scientists or whole human beings. It is impossible to persuade the scientist that he ought to elect to make every man a free, full-flowering, active, self-expressing savant except on the ground that every man should be enabled to give full expression to his natural faculties, actual or only possible. But that argument above all is without merit for the purpose because it presupposes human nature and the flowering of human nature as we know it, while the scientist lives for the transcendence of that nature and is in fact necessarily indecisive as to what sort of nature he ought to implant in man in place of that which now exists.

To determine whether natural science implies a standard of moral obligation is not a school exercise but a matter of grave political concern; and whether it implies a moral obligation in the greater toward the less is precisely one of the points on which we must satisfy ourselves if we are to have any confidence that our programs of foreign aid are neither marred by stinginess nor founded on weak sentimentality. Science, which has had so much to do with shaping our times, has as its principle and epitome, Knowledge is Power. No generation has had clearer ocular evidence than ours has to show that there is nothing in science itself that tends to limit the direction or extent of its own development. Surely no one will undertake to say what miracles will have been performed, barring catastrophes, in a century; and in a millennium, the Creation replicated. Nothing intrinsic to science or power limits or prescribes the use to which power is put, as we can prove to ourselves if we consider the standing of an agent made omnicompetent by his omnisapience.

Toward whom could the omnicompetent re-creator of nature be thought to have a duty, and what would be the ground for the existence of a duty binding such a being? He could be imagined to have a duty to his prospective creatures, that is, to the whole of human and non-human being about to take shape under his hands. We see how problematic the existence of such a duty is when we try to understand what the omnicompetent agent would be bound to perform, and why or how, being omnicompetent, he could be bound. As to the first part of the question, it might be thought that the Agent has a duty to make a good world, consisting of good men and a proper inanimate environment to support or encourage their goodness. We shall not stop to try to understand what could be meant by a good world. It is hard enough to understand the goodness of parts, which can be judged by how well they are articulated to form a whole; but to judge the whole, we have perhaps nothing to fall back on but existence itself: the whole is good if it exists, that is, if it is not destroyed by internal contradictions. Since it is not open to human scientists to bring the whole into being, their project for the perfect conquest of nature is perhaps not to be construed absolutely or literally. Still, the question of the standard of goodness for the beings they can re-form persists. We shall not try to answer it; our problem is, does the omnicompetent agent have a duty to make his objects one way rather than another—say, free rather than servile—or to put them into one state of being rather than another, for their advantage.

Duty as moral obligation is a bond upon those for whom there exists an "other" that matters. Why does the "other" matter? Either by prescription of law laid down by a greater power; or because of a calculation of the benefit of the one acting; or gratuitously out of the desire of the one acting. But a duty of the omnicompetent scientist to his objects cannot follow from the legislation of a greater power than omnicompetence as such, for there is none. Nor can the dictate of the agent's benefit be called a ground of duty; the proper name for that motive is calculation. Nor is the gratuitous desire of the powerful agent the ground of his duty; on the contrary, what is done gratuitously is by that very fact not done out of the right of the patient or out of any duty binding the agent.

Thus it follows that if science means the conquest of nature, and knowledge is the power of conquering nature, then the possession of scientific knowledge as such carries with it no *duty* to improve man's condition but only a possibility of doing so. Their possession of science does not impose a duty upon the advanced nations to assist the others. This is not to say that the powerful and prosperous ought not to succor the weak and wretched, but that the latter have no right growing out of a duty in the former, imposed upon them by their power and prosperity, to benefit the backward.

### III

Fortunately for the cause of philanthropy, the fact that there is not implicit in the power of science a restraining duty to the unscientific need not mean that the power of science is restrained by nothing at all. On the contrary, precisely because the power of science is presumed (by science) to reach indefinitely far in all directions, it does not reach in one direction rather than another. Since the improvement of man's condition is a meaningless phrase unless it rests upon clear notions of the difference between making conditions better and making them worse, the power to make the human condition better must be guided by men who possess knowledge of the difference between better and worse for human beings. But that knowledge is of the sort needed by men who direct other men's actions; it is the knowledge needed by legislators. Scientists as such must, as in practice they do, come under law, under human law, under human legislators, and thus under political authority. Scientists or the ministers of supreme physical power are under the jurisdiction of political authority; science itself is or may be brought under that authority, for science is an activity of human beings. Therefore the possibility exists that out of the ascendancy of politics over science, as of the human over the subhuman, a duty arises that causes the power over nature to activate an engine of beneficence.

We cannot here take up in its own right the question how far science can or must be brought under political prudence. But we are entitled to make this purely deductive remark: All those who refuse to live with the conclusion that science leads to no duty of benevolence, and who then turn to the ascendancy of political judgment over scientific power, must then recognize that they have conceded the insufficiency of the broad scientific project as it conceives itself; and that they have done so because science provides powerful means but gives no humane guidance as to ends. Liberal-minded men who find themselves dissatisfied with the scientific outlook are in fact dissatisfied with the moral neutrality of science. It may be assumed that they are a fortiori dissatisfied with that scientization of social science that deprives even political science of the moral content appropriate to it, more emphatically than science proper is so deprived.

Instead of the general question, Does the political control of science imply that the monopolists of science have a duty to relieve the estate of the backward, we will confine ourselves to the more limited question of United States policy, in the following form: Is there something in the nature of democracy that imposes a duty of universal beneficence upon a democratic nation?

The answer seems implicit in the words of the Declaration of Independence: "We hold these truths to be self-evident, that all men are created equal, that they are endowed by their Creator with certain inalienable Rights, that among these are Life, Liberty, and the pursuit of Happiness." We govern ourselves, only a part of mankind, by the light of a principle that we assert to be true of all mankind. We appeal to nature and the nature of man and to the laws of nature, and by that same appeal we appeal to the single humanity of men everywhere. The bond of equality among all men is made the bond of equality among Americans. If the natural equality of all men is the constituting principle of democracy, then perhaps it is wrong for us to enjoy prosperity while others, our equals, are in adversity, to be well fed while others are hungry, to live out our three score years and ten while others are destined at birth to perish before the prime of life. The ruling principle of democracy encompasses all humanity; men may be excused for supposing that the ruling principle of democracy imposes upon democrats a duty to all humanity.

It must be allowed that the great Declaration does not dwell upon moral duties, nor does it emphasize the transcendent unity of mankind in opposition to the dividedness of mankind into nations. The Declaration is a statement of rights, not of duties; the only duty mentioned is the duty that men have to enforce their natural rights when other men violate them. And assuredly the Declaration is an announcement of political independence, of emphatic distinctness from the rest of mankind: "separate and equal" is the language of the Declaration to describe the station of Americans among the nations. The equality of all men in their natural rights is of no practical effect until there is political society to put those rights in steady execution: "to secure these Rights, Governments are instituted among Men." Democracy is a form of government, it emphatically presupposes political life and therewith the division of the world into nations. It does not view man directly as a natural being, a member of a species, over the barriers so to speak of conventional distinction. Democracy recognizes, as it could not exist without recognizing, the difference between fellow-citizens and aliens. Thus wherever the Constitution pronounces that certain things may or shall not be done, it means they may or shall not be done where the Constitution has authority; it lays down the law primarily to Americans as such. Democracy, in brief, is a form of government, a political regime predicated upon the belief that the enjoyment of the natural or universal rights depends on the conventional, political particularization of mankind into separate, viable bodies, namely, nations, under government. Democracy is not a basis for the amalgamation of the human kind into one mass and it neither depends upon nor leads up to a fundamental moral duty.

Whether or not it is paradoxical, it is yet true that the democratic teaching of the Declaration begins with natural equality but does so in order to conserve conventional inequality, for example, inequality of wealth and inequality of political authority, which is what is meant by government. The democratic teaching of the Declaration and the Constitution contains nothing that is intended to afflict the conscience of wealth or power lawfully obtained and employed. True as this is in the relations of fellow-citizens one with another, it is a fortiori true in respect of the rest of the world.

If we were compelled to speculate on the reason that our democratic principles are so free from the taint of misdirected egalitarianism, we might look for the answer in some writings of the draftsman of the Declaration. In his *Notes on the State of Virginia* (toward the end of Query XIV), Jefferson describes a scheme for the competitive, progressively selective education of the young. His plan would operate by passing the students upward through a school system that sifted them and reduced their numbers drastically as they moved from one stage to the next higher. By means of these dismissals, "the best geniuses will be raked from the rubbish annually." Jefferson speaks freely of boys (not boys and girls) of "superior parts" and "superior genius." The natural equality that is intrinsic to our democratic principles is not all-inclusive. It coexists with natural inequalities of the sort that Jefferson knew and that we know will assert themselves in every classroom. The fundamental principles of democracy do not contemplate an undifferentiated humanity. It is impossible to infer from the classic democracy of the Declaration of Independence and the Constitution of the United States a duty to mankind, partly because it is impossible to infer from that democracy a limitless egalitarianism. Our fundamental democratic principles depreciate neither certain natural nor certain conventional inequalities. In other words our democratic equalitarianism is political, not universalistic.

It is not to be supposed that every group or nation constituted by a universal principle (such as that all men are created equal) is obliged by the universality of its principle as if by a moral duty to all men. This becomes clear when we consider our moral duty to beings who are undoubtedly men, but who are not ruled by our universal principle, or who indeed are ruled by an antithetic universal principle. It is evident that we do not have a moral duty to extend foreign aid to Red China, and the reason is that their universal principle would destroy ours. In the same way, churches do not always take seriously the argument that, because they teach the fatherhood of God and the brotherhood of man, they have a duty to comfort pagans, heretics, or even schismatics as such. The reason for this is not obscure: the goodness or truth of each universal principle implies the goodness of the practical influence of that principle upon living, acting men. It is not possible rationally to believe in the goodness of democracy and at the same time to interpret democracy as if it implies a duty that is destructive of democracy by being antithetic to the existence of democratic nations as such. If democracy implies a moral duty of any kind, it is to cultivate those qualities suited to keep democracies alive, which is as much as to say, it obliges us to preserve ourselves.

A very small nation may be constituted by a very large principle. Ancient Israel was petty as a nation; its constitution was vastly comprehensive. It is wrong and dangerous to suppose that the universality of our democratic principle obliges or even entitles us to act toward other men as if our universal principle had universal applicability. In order to make it possible for us to act toward all men as if our universal principle were in force or had authority among all men, it would be necessary for us to extend our rule over all men or at least to propagate democracy among them universally. What duty that might spring from the goodness of democracy could exceed in vitality the duty to spread the source of that goodness, democracy itself, to every corner of the earth? The danger and the infeasibility of such imperialism in the name of a theory is proved through the conduct of our adversaries, who also subscribe to certain universal propositions, assertions about all men, and who wish to act upon those principles toward all men. Inevitably we and others resist. Resistance is inevitable because there are many—how many is hard to say— universal propositions, assertions about all men, that can be maintained and that might even be true. That all men are created equal is one universal principle; that they incline toward the good is another; and that they are determined in their natures by their material conditions is a third. If political life and therewith national "duties" are to be founded upon each nation's extension in practice of its own universal theory, there will be no alternative but for diplomacy to turn into dialectic or war. The former is impossible, the latter undesirable. The conclusion is that we must be content to cultivate our own democratic vineyard and to sit in the shade of our constitutional doctrines without imagining that, because the Thirteenth Amendment follows from a truth about all men, it is *ipso facto* the guide to our action upon all men. It is not and cannot be so; it does and is meant to govern the conduct of Americans toward other Americans, of men who owe allegiance to the Constitution. It has literally no meaning if read in any other sense.

This is not to say that the nation must not act in defense of its life principle. On the contrary, it must so act; the Declaration teaches this as a duty. But there is no such thing as a duty implicit in democracy to act democratically in defense of democracy. Therefore the government's actions in defense of democracy have the essential character of deeds done in the interest of living democracy, that is, of democratic nations; they do not in principle have the character of deeds done out of a universal duty inferred from the universal principle that lies at the heart of democracy.

The foregoing has been intended to show that the democracy of the great Declaration and of the Constitution does not imply or presuppose the radical unity of the human race in such a sense as to impose duties of beneficence upon the prosperous. Neither its substantive teaching as to equality nor the formal universality of that teaching makes it possible to deduce from our democratic principle such a duty as would convert science into an engine of universal beneficence under the tutelage of democracy.

## IV

It is very difficult to demonstrate, either from the sentiment of charity, or from the significance of the scientific project for the melioration of man's estate, or from the principles of democracy itself, that there is a duty to relieve the wretched, or that adversity has a moral right to be succored by prosperity. It is even more difficult to obliterate from the human heart a fellow-feeling with fellow-men, a sense of compassion for the pains of other beings and, indeed, even of sympathy with their pleasures to some extent. Certainly compassion for the pains of others can be explained as the result of our putting ourselves in the place of the sufferers, of our imagining pain and then weakly experiencing it in some form. To explain compassion in this way is to imply that what we do to relieve the sufferer we do in order to remove a cause of pain in ourselves. Acting so is to obey something different from the dictate of moral duty. Nevertheless, however human sympathy may be explained or explained away, men who lack it are doubtless capable of the most extreme brutality, for they feel nothing for their victims and can therefore give way to the cruelest passions. At the very least, compassion acts as a bond among men, heightened when the beautiful, the well-endowed, or the eminent suffer; stimulated by the sights and sounds of agony but soothed by an aversion of the eyes and a stopping of the ears; weakened by the competition of self-interest; diminished to nothing by long habituation as in sport arenas, in abattoirs, at the scaffold, on fields of battle, or even in hospitals of mercy; and capable of being distracted and turned into its opposite by indignation or the appetite for revenge.

# The Right of Foreign Aid

Compassion is not itself the basis for the unity of the human race, but it reminds us of the fact of that unity. Our question whether there is a duty to extend aid abroad cannot be answered unless we can give an account of that unity, determining at last whether we are all one in such a sense that, in principle, the blessings of the few belong in part to the unblessed many, or whether we are one in some other sense. Now it is self-evident that the human race is a unity that consists of parts or elements, and it is evident from our having to discuss foreign aid that some parts are in a condition to which the others aspire, but not vice versa. Whether one civilization more truly deserves the name than does another is surely a difficult question, one that we need not answer here; but we cannot abstain from noting that the question of the difference in the levels of civilization is implicit in the wish of some nations to resemble others or to resemble them in some respects, and also in the opinion that prevails among the advanced that they should share the basis or the fruits of their progress with the backward. Some nations must borrow the means and arts of war and subsistence, other nations are compelled to draw on foreigners for the theoretical goods. We will not try to say whether being a receiver in one of these senses is outweighed by being a giver in the other. But we can say with ease and certainty that to be a receiver in both senses is the mark of being in a backward state of civilization. Manifestly the human race is a unity as it is distinguished from everything non-human, just as each family is a unit in distinction to everything outside it. But within each family there is an unmistakable subordination and superordination of the members, and similarly in the articulated unity of the human kind as a whole. Surely all the members of a family are equal in belonging to the human race; but they are unequal in so many other respects that it would be absurd to speak only of the duties of parents and the rights of children, never of the duties of the subordinate members and the prerogatives of the more competent. The duties are different on the one side from those on the other: the duties of providing and educating on the side of superior competence, and the duties of obedience and helpfulness on the other side. Those who would persuade us that there is a duty to extend foreign aid can scarcely expect to succeed as long as they appear to argue that that duty carries with it no corresponding prerogative on our part nor a correlative duty on the part of the nations whose condition compels them to sue for assistance. It is false and harmful to argue from subordination and superordination as the grounds of duty in the superior, and then to deny all other consequences because they do not flatter our undiscriminating prejudices.

The distinction between those imagined to have a duty to extend help and those who, being backward, need it is the distinction between those who stand at a certain stage of life and those who hope to be set in motion toward it. It is elementary that every thing which is in a state of change should be discussed and treated in the light of where it is at the moment, as well as by reference to what it might some day be. The child who is treated as if he were already wise is at a disadvantage in comparison with the child who is treated as if he is now ignorant but may be impelled toward a better state. Only by a compounding of cant and illogic can it be asserted that the difference between greater and less must positively be eradicated and is at the same time of no significance. If it be thought that the practical consequence of such notions is a tutelage of the lesser to the greater, then that possibility must be faced; and though it be granted that such a state would be deplorable, yet it would be as nothing in comparison with the effects of a doctrinaire abdication by the greater of their wealth, their influence, and eventually their fate to the concourse of rude and barely emergent humanity.

Men wish it were possible to treat with potentiality as if it were actuality, with childhood as if it were maturity, with cannibals as if they were citizens, with what is not as if it were. To act so is to give way to self-deception and to deny that there is a necessity in things to which we must bend our wills, however freely we may exercise them after acknowledging the ascendancy of that necessity.

To appeal to necessity is not to make a ground for renouncing the discipline of moral obligation. By a too simple view, necessity can be made synonymous with the demand of self-preservation, and then a man who preserves himself by deserting his friends, betraying his country, and sheltering behind a parapet of his heaped-up victims can be exculpated by the rule of necessity. Worse yet, the man who murders in a blinding rage or from the prompting of a cruel and perverted nature could be said to act from necessity and thus to be exempt from blame and punishment. We must evidently discriminate the end to which necessity is properly directed if we are to avoid criminal mistakes, for it is not enough that vice is necessary for a bad man's pleasure, that he be exonerated or even encouraged.

I take it that "to be" or to continue to be is the impulse and tendency of everything that is; and that a thing most emphatically is when it is self-sufficient, or as little as possible exposed to being put out of existence because of the presence or absence of something alien to itself. Moreover, a thing "is" more emphatically or more completely when it is capable of all the acts that one of its type can in principle attain to: a dog is more a dog with four legs than with three, and with a courageous heart than without one. This double meaning of "to be" is reflected in the double meaning of "perfect": complete in itself, and excellently good. I take it to be necessary or of the nature of necessity that things and men strive to be in this double sense.

To obey necessity and thus to seek the means of their being is the law of the nature of men and nations. The precept of that law is delivered in tones that ring with the call to duty. To be bound to the necessary means to shun superfluity and insufficiency. Men deviate from the necessary when they fail to make prudent provision and when they wallow in a surfeit. To kill wantonly is to kill superfluously, unnecessarily, and therefore to commit an act of vice. Gossip differs from testimony in that it is gratuitous, there is no reason for it; and it generally earns contempt. When an act is unnecessary, there is no reason for it or behind it. The things men do for which they do not strictly speaking have a reason are strictly speaking not reasonable. This does not mean they originate without a cause. It means they originate from an unreasonable cause: envy, lust, malice, megalomania, avarice, or any one of a baker's dozen. The rational and the moral find a common ground in the necessary: the avoidance of the insufficient, the superfluous, and the inessential or untrue. From this maxim we learn our duty with respect to the backward or the simply needy.

We have indeed a duty as a nation not to deprave ourselves in a glut of baubles; and as citizens, not to decay into a brawling pack which spends its manliness in squabbling over the same baubles. It is not immoral to provide for oneself; it is immoral to provide in ways that are at the same time repulsive and incapacitating. Our duty to lighten the load of human misery is derivative from, indeed it is the reflex of our duty to bear ourselves as a great nation—firmly to wield a mighty power in a mighty cause. Liberally we must feed those mouths that will not confuse the hand with the aliment; grimly we must struggle against suffocation in our own abundance; and confidently we must draw the connection between liberality and authority. Grandeur has liberality as a sign, authority as a prerogative. That is the ground and the right of foreign aid.

*Basis for truth of foreign aid : Because we are a great power*

# President John F. Kennedy

●

# FOREIGN AID, 1963*

*To the Congress of the United States:*

"Peace hath her victories no less renowned than war," wrote
Milton. And no peace-time victory in history has been as far-
reaching in its impact, nor served the cause of freedom so well,
as the victories scored in the last 17 years by this nation's mutual
defense and assistance programs. These victories have been, in
the main, quiet instead of dramatic. Their aim has been, not to
gain territories for the United States or support in the United
Nations, but to preserve freedom and hope, and to prevent tyranny
and subversion, in dozens of key nations all over the world.

The United States today is spending over 10 per cent of its
gross national product on programs primarily aimed at improving
our national security. Somewhat less than 1-20th of this amount,
and less than 0.7 per cent of our gross national product, goes
into the mutual assistance program: Roughly half for economic
development, and half for military and other short-term assistance. The contribution of this program to our national interest
clearly outweighs its cost. The richest nation in the world would
surely be justified in spending less than 1 per cent of its national
income on assistance to its less fortunate sister nations solely as
a matter of international responsibility; but inasmuch as these
programs are not merely the right thing to do, but clearly in our
national self-interest, all criticisms should be placed in that perspective. That our aid programs can be improved is not a matter
of debate. But that our aid programs serve both our national
traditions and our national interests is beyond all reasonable
doubt.

*Selections from the Message of the President to the Congress, on the
subject of foreign aid, transmitted on April 2, 1963. Reprinted from *The New
York Times*, April 3, 1963.

## President John F. Kennedy

History records that our aid programs to Turkey and Greece were the crucial element that enabled Turkey to stand up against heavy-handed Soviet pressures, Greece to put down Communist aggression, and both to re-create stable societies and to move forward in the direction of economic and social growth.

History records that the Marshall Plan made it possible for the nations of Western Europe, including the United Kingdom, to recover from the devastation of the world's most destructive war, to rebuild military strength, to withstand the expansionist thrust of Stalinist Russia, and to embark on an economic renaissance which has made Western Europe the second greatest and richest industrial complex in the world today—a vital center of free world strength, itself now contributing to the growth and strength of less developed countries.

History records that our military and economic assistance to nations on the frontiers of the Communist world—such as Iran, Pakistan, India, Vietnam and Free China—has enabled threatened peoples to stay free and independent, when they otherwise would have either been overrun by aggressive Communist power or fallen victim of utter chaos, poverty and despair.

History records that our contributions to international aid have been the critical factor in the growth of a whole family of international financial institutions and agencies, playing an ever more important role in the ceaseless war against want and the struggle for growth and freedom.

And finally, history will record that today our technical assistance and development loans are giving hope where hope was lacking, sparking action where life was static, and stimulating progress around the earth—simultaneously supporting the military security of the free world, helping to erect barriers against the growth of Communism where those barriers count the most, helping to build the kind of world community of independent, self-supporting nations in which we want to live, and helping to serve the deep American urge to extend a generous hand to those working toward a better life for themselves and their children.

Despite noisy opposition from the very first days—despite dire predictions that foreign aid would "bankrupt" the republic —despite warnings that the Marshall Plan and successor programs were "throwing our money down a rat-hole"—despite great practical difficulties and some mistakes and disappointments—the fact is that our aid programs generally and consistently have done what they were expected to do.

Freedom is not on the run anywhere in the world—not in Europe, Asia, Africa, or Latin America—as it might well have been without United States aid. And we now know that freedom —all freedom, including our own—is diminished when other countries fall under Communist domination, as in China in 1949, North Vietnam and the northern provinces of Laos in 1954, and Cuba in 1959. Freedom, all freedom, is threatened by the subtle, varied and unceasing Communist efforts at subversion in Latin America, Africa, the Middle East, and Asia. And the prospect for freedom is also endangered or eroded in countries which see no hope—no hope for a better life based on economic progress, education, social justice and the development of stable institutions. These are the frontiers of freedom which our military and economic aid programs seek to advance; and in so doing, they serve our deepest national interest.

This view has been held by three successive Presidents— Democratic and Republican alike. It has been endorsed by a bipartisan majority of nine successive Congresses. It has been supported for 17 years by a bipartisan majority of the American people.

And it has only recently been reconfirmed by a distinguished committee of private citizens, headed by General Lucius Clay . . . . Their report stated: "We believe these programs, properly conceived and implemented, to be essential to the security of our nation and necessary to the exercise of its world-wide responsibilities."

There is, in short, a national concensus of many years standing on the vital importance of these programs. The principle and purpose of United States assistance to less secure and less fortunate nations are not and cannot be seriously in doubt.

The question now is: What about the future? In the perspective of these past gains, what is the dimension of present needs, what are our opportunities, and what changes do we face at this juncture in world history?

## President John F. Kennedy

I believe it is a crucial juncture. Our world is near the climax of an historic convulsion. A tidal wave of national independence has nearly finished its sweep through lands which contain one out of every three people in the world. The industrial and scientific revolution is spreading to the far corners of the earth. And two irreconcilable views of the value, the rights and the role of the individual human being confront the peoples of the world.

In some 80 developing nations, countless large and small decisions will be made in the days and months and years ahead —decisions which, taken together, will establish the economic and social system, determine the political leadership, shape the political practices, and mold the structure of the institutions which will promote either consent or coercion for one-third of humanity. And these decisions will drastically affect the shape of the world in which our children grow to maturity.

Africa is stirring restlessly to consolidate its independence and to make that independence meaningful for its people through economic and social development. The people of America have affirmed and reaffirmed their sympathy with these objectives.

Free Asia is responding resolutely to the political, economic and military challenge of Communist China's relentless efforts to dominate the continent.

Latin America is striving to take decisive steps toward effective democracy—amid the turbulence of rapid social change and the menace of Communist subversion.

The United States—the richest and most powerful of all peoples, a nation committed to the independence of nations and to a better life for all peoples—can no more stand aside in this climactic age of decision than we can withdraw from the community of free nations. Our effort is not merely symbolic. It is addressed to our vital security interests.

It is in this context that I hope the American people through their representatives in Congress will consider our request for foreign aid funds designed carefully and explicitly to meet these specific challenges. This is not a wearisome burden. It is a new chapter in our involvement in a continuously vital struggle—the most challenging and constructive effort ever undertaken by man on behalf of freedom and his fellow man.

# Foreign Aid, 1963

## OBJECTIVES

In a changing world, our programs of mutual defense and assistance must be kept under constant review. My recommendations herein reflect the work of the Clay committee, the scrutiny undertaken by the new administrator of the Agency for International Development, and the experience gained in our first full year of administering the new and improved program enacted by the Congress in 1961. There is fundamental agreement throughout these reviews: That these assistance programs are of great value to our deepest national interest—that their basic concepts and organization, as embodied in the existing legislation, are properly conceived—that progress has been made and is being made in translating these concepts into action—but that much still remains to be done to improve our performance and make the best possible use of these programs.

In addition, there is fundamental agreement in all these reviews regarding six key recommendations for the future.

*Objective No. 1:* To apply stricter standards of selectivity and self-help in aiding developing countries. . . .

Considerable progress has already been made along these lines. While the number of former colonies achieving independence has lengthened the total list of countries receiving assistance, 80 per cent of all economic assistance now goes to only 30 countries; and military assistance is even more narrowly concentrated. The proportion of development loans, as contrasted with outright grants, has increased from 10 per cent to 60 per cent. We have placed all our development lending on a dollar repayable basis; and this year we are increasing our efforts, as the Clay committee recommended, to tailor our loan terms so that interest rates and maturities will reflect to a greater extent the differences in the ability of different countries to service debt.

In the Alliance for Progress in particular, and increasingly in other aid programs, emphasis is placed upon self-help and self-reform by the recipients themselves, using our aid as a catalyst for progress and not as a handout. Finally, in addition to emphasizing primarily economic rather than military assistance, wherever conditions permit, we are taking a sharp new look at both the size and purpose of those local military forces which receive our assistance. Our increased stress on internal security and civic action in military assistance is in keeping with our experience that in developing countries, military forces can have an important economic as well as protective role to play. . . .

*Objective No. 2:* To achieve a reduction and ultimate elimination of United States assistance by enabling nations to stand on their own as rapidly as possible. Both this nation and the countries we help have a stake in their reaching the point of self-sustaining growth—the point where they no longer require external aid to maintain their independence. Our goal is not an arbitrary cutoff date but the earliest possible "takeoff" date—the date when their economies will have been launched with sufficient momentum to enable them to become self-supporting, requiring only the same normal sources of external financing to meet expanding capital needs that this country required for many decades. . . .

The record clearly shows that foreign aid is not an endless or unchanging process. Fifteen years ago our assistance went almost entirely to the advanced countries of Europe and Japan —today it is directed almost entirely to the developing world. Ten years ago most of our assistance was given to shoring up military forces and unstable economies—today this kind of aid has been cut in half, and our assistance goes increasingly toward economic development. There are still, however, important cases where there has been no diminution in the Communist military threat, and both military and economic aid are still required. Such cases range from relatively stabilized frontiers, as in Korea and Turkey, to areas of active aggression, such as Vietnam.

*Objective No. 3:* To secure the increased participation of other industrialized nations in sharing the cost of international development assistance. . . .

*Objective No. 4:* To lighten any adverse impact of the aid program on our own balance of payments and economy. . . .

*Objective No. 5:* To continue to assist in the defense of countries under threat of external and internal Communist attack. Our military assistance program has been an essential element in keeping the boundary of Soviet and Chinese military power relatively stable for over a decade. Without its protection the substantial economic progress made by underdeveloped countries along the Sino-Soviet periphery would hardly have been possible.

As these countries build economic strength, they will be able to assume more of the burden of their defense. But we must not assume that military assistance to these countries—or to others primarily exposed to subversive internal attack—can be ended in the foreseeable future. On the contrary, while it will be possible to reduce and terminate some programs, we should anticipate the need for new and expanded programs.

India is a case in point. The wisdom of earlier United States aid in helping the Indian subcontinent's considerable and fruitful efforts toward progress and stability can hardly now be in question. The threat made plain by the Chinese attack on India last fall may require additional efforts on our part to help bolster the security of this crucial area, assuming these efforts can be matched in an appropriate way by the efforts of India and Pakistan.

But overall, the magnitude of military assistance is small in relation to our national security expenditures; in this fiscal year it amounts to about 3 per cent of our defense budget. "Dollar for dollar," said the Clay committee with particular reference to the border areas, "these programs contribute more to the security of the free world than corresponding expenditures in our defense appropriations. . . . These countries are providing more than 2 million armed men ready, for the most part, for an emergency." Clearly, if this program did not exist, our defense budget would undoubtedly have to be increased substantially to provide an equivalent contribution to the free world's defense.

*Objective No. 6:* To increase the role of private investment and other non-Federal resources in assisting developing nations. . . .

## ALLIANCE FOR PROGRESS

In a special sense, the achievements of the Alliance for Progress in the coming years will be the measure of our determination, our ideals, and our wisdom. Here in this hemisphere, in this last year, our resourcefulness as a people was challenged in the clearest terms. We moved at once to resist the threat of aggressive nuclear weapons in Cuba, and we found the nations of Latin America at our side. They, like ourselves, were brought to a new awareness of the danger of permitting the poverty and despair of a whole people to continue long anywhere in this continent.

Had the needs of the people of Cuba been met in the pre-

Castro period—their need for food, for housing, for education, for jobs, above all, for a democratic responsibility in the fulfillment of their own hopes—there would have been no Castro, no missiles in Cuba, and no need for Cuba's neighbors to incur the immense risks of resistance to threatened aggression from that island.

There is but one way to avoid being faced with similar dilemmas in the future. It is to bring about in all the countries of Latin America the conditions of hope, in which the peoples of this continent will know that they can shape a better future for themselves, not through obeying the inhuman commands of an alien and cynical ideology, but through personal self-expression, individual judgment, and the acts of responsible citizenship.

As Americans, we have long recognized the legitimacy of these aspirations; in recent months we have been able to see, as never before, their urgency and, I believe, the concrete means for their realization.

In less than two years the 10-year program of the Alliance for Progress has become more than an idea and more than a commitment of governments. The necessary initial effort to develop plans, to organize institutions, to test and experiment has itself required and achieved a new dedication—a new dedication to intelligent compromise between old and new ways of life. In the long run, it is this effort—and not the threat of Communism—that will determine the fate of freedom in the Western Hemisphere.

These years have not been easy ones for any group in Latin America. A similar change in the fundamental orientation of our own society would have been no easier. The difficulty of the changes to be brought about makes all the more heartening the success of many nations of Latin America in achieving reforms which will make their fundamental economic and social structures both more efficient and more equitable. . . .

Since 1961, eleven Latin-American countries—Argentina, Bolivia, Brazil, Colombia, Chile, Costa Rica, the Dominican Republic, El Salvador, Mexico, Panama, and Venezuela—have made structural reforms in their tax systems. Twelve countries have improved their income tax laws and administration.

New large-scale programs for improved land use and land reform have been undertaken in Venezuela, the Dominican Republic and two states in Brazil. More limited plans are being carried out in Chile, Colombia, Panama, Uruguay and Central America.

Six Latin-American countries—Colombia, Chile, Bolivia, Honduras, Mexico, and Venezuela—have submitted development programs to the panel of experts of the Organization of American States. The panel has evaluated and reported on the first three and will soon offer its views on the balance.

Viewed against the background of decades of neglect—or, at most, intermittent bursts of attention to basic problems—the start that has been made is encouraging. Perhaps most significant of all is a change in the hearts and minds of the people—a growing will to develop their countries. We can only help Latin Americans to save themselves. It is for this reason that the increasing determination of the peoples of the region to build modern societies is heartening. And it is for this reason that responsible leadership in Latin America must respond to this popular will with a greater sense of urgency and purpose, lest aspirations turn into frustrations and hope turn into despair. Pending reform legislation must be enacted, statutes already on the books must be enforced, and mechanisms for carrying out programs must be organized and invigorated. These steps are not easy, as we know from our own experience, but they must be taken.

Our own intention is to concentrate our support in Latin America on those countries adhering to the principles established in the Charter of Punta del Este, and to work with our neighbors to indicate more precisely the particular policy changes, reforms and other self-help measures which are necessary to make our assistance effective and the Alliance a success. . . .

A beginning has been made in the first two years of the Alliance; but the job that is still ahead must be tackled with continuing urgency. Many of the ingredients for a successful decade are at hand, and the fundamental course for the future is clear. It remains for all parties to the Alliance to provide the continuous will and effort needed to move steadily along that course. . . .

### Conclusion

In closing, let me again emphasize the overriding importance of the efforts in which we are engaged.

## President John F. Kennedy

At this point in history we can look back to many successes in the struggle to preserve freedom. Our nation is still daily winning unseen victories in the fight against Communist subversion in the slums and hamlets, in the hospitals and schools, and in the offices of governments across a world bent on lifting itself. Two centuries of pioneering and growth must be telescoped into decades and even years. This is a field of action for which our history has prepared us, to which our aspirations have drawn us, and into which our national interest moves us.

Around the world cracks in the monolithic apparatus of our adversary are there for all to see. This, for the American people, is a time for vision, for patience, for work and for wisdom. For better or worse, we are the pacesetters. Freedom's leader cannot flag or falter, or another runner will set the pace.

We have dared to label the sixties the decade of development. But it is not the eloquence of our slogans, but the quality of our endurance, which will determine whether this generation of Americans deserves the leadership which history has thrust upon us.

PRINTED IN U.S.A.